AF573690

The West Country from the Sea

"Say Mister, wot 'appens if we turn right – up 'ere?"

The West Country from the Sea

Lyme Bay to Land's End

David and Joan Hay

EDWARD STANFORD LONDON

Edward Stanford Limited
12-14 Long Acre, London WC2E 9LP
First Published 1972

Printed in Great Britain by
Lowe & Brydone (Printers) Limited

ISBN 540 00957 1

Acknowledgements

I cannot help feeling we should really be acknowledging our indebtedness to that great panorama of colour and cloud shadow that goes to make up the West Country with its great harbours and deep bays – and without which there would have been no book. Or perhaps we should say 'thank you' to the birds who set still anchorages alight not only with song but with a life which all our knowledge is powerless to corrupt and insufficient to understand.

But perhaps they wouldn't get the message, so may I just say how grateful we were to our old friends Bill and Janet Moss and Stafford East whose knowledge of the West Country and its pubs was invaluable. R.F.S. Orchard was very helpful about the Exe and we are grateful to John Bolingbroke for his kindly help as to recent developments – over a noggin in *The Dolphin* at Newton Ferrers – and how delighted we were to lunch with our old B.B.C. colleagues Tony and Audrey Wigan who have now returned to the Dart from the New World.

Lastly, though he is long since dead, I should like to raise a glass to Commander Lampard with whom, in those far off days before the war, I first explored the Devon waters.

Contents

Illustrations

Introduction

I cannot set a course for the West Country without a whole host of complicating emotions crowding in. I shall always find it difficult – almost impossible – to differentiate logically between my actual physical acquaintance with the rock strewn bars of Salcombe or the Avon sand banks, and the still vivid memories of a colourful King Arthur charging at the head of his knights across the enchanted pages of my nursery books. The trouble is, I think, that the early recollections of improbable romance stick more hauntingly than the more prosaic realities of later life.

A child's imagination needs something small and simple which it can understand and upon which it can readily build its own colourful imagery. Unlike over educated grown-ups, he is not in the least put off by unlikely suits of mediaeval armour adorning early Celtic knights. My father was a wonderful teller of the stories of myth and legend and so, as soon as I began to wander off on my own, each nook and cranny became alive in my imagination.

A little hollow in a Roman stone quarry, floored with thyme and wild marjoram and fringed with the crimson heather bell became the entrance to King Arthur's hide-out or Merlin's hermitage from where, when the gusty wind dropped momentarily, you would almost hear the war trumpet of Sir Bors as he rallied his tired horsemen. There were no inhibitions in those days – even the Norns and Valkyries got mixed up in the gales that thundered up the seaward estuaries.

Sadly, I have to admit now as I sit at the tiller, that the Arthurian legend is probably one of the most engaging pieces of pure fiction that has ever coloured our island history. Nennius, who revised the first book on this period, the *Historia Britronum* of 811 A.D. only mentions a local *Dux Bellorum* who led the Cornish

Britons against the Saxon invaders of Devon, and it is left to the highly imaginative Geoffrey of Monmouth in the twelfth century to collect together the fragments of the Arthurian legend as we know it today. He is followed by the fifteenth century English translator Malory in his *Morte d'Arthur,* though the Mabinogian doesn't even give Arthur a mention.

Having, as in duty bound, given you the prosaic facts, I must admit that Cornwall for me will always be the 'Land of Saints and fairies' that lies, as Tennyson says in his *Morte d'Arthur,* between 'the great deep and the great deep' in 'the stillness of the dead world's winter dawn,' and I shall remember Sir Bedivere, the first and last of the knights, climbing that highest cliff, from where he saw, or thought he saw, the speck that bore the King,

'Down that long water, opening on the deep
Somewhere far off, pass on, and on and go
From less to less and vanish into light.'

I would hate to think in this computerised age of power cuts and political journalism that we

'Shall never more at any future time
Delight our souls with talk of knightly deeds,
Walking about the gardens and the halls
Of Camelot, as in the days that were.'

But the rewarding part of cruising in this West Country is that you can't escape this 'talk of knightly deeds' all down the centuries. Is it not the land of Drake and Frobisher and all the Elizabethan sea captains who managed to combine profitable piracy with patriotic fervour while sowing the seeds of the most astonishing Empire a little island has ever put together by chance conquest?

There is a quite unexpected variety about this stretch of coast that we yachtsmen so often tend to lump together as one entity. You will find it is three quite distinct countries. Much of Dorset is pockety and snug and in the hollows of its chalk hills lies all that the heart of man could reasonably wish for, mild climate, kindly soil and the modest grace of grey villages in sheltered valleys; the leisurely communion of down and ancient woods. I always think of it as the land of blue vinny and fabulous cricket teas.

Deep meadowed Devon is a land of shady creeks and cider mills and old stone farms nestling under the moorland hills where the slow speech of the Saxon still pleases the ear of the traveller. Theirs is an unhurried life where there is still time to finish that game of bowls and dowse the strawberries in clotted cream!

I know there is no barbed wire fence between Devon and Cornwall but the most insensitive man cannot fail to notice that he has crossed over into the land of Celtic twilight – the land of the 'little people' and giants and warlocks and faintly suspicious locals who still look askance at 'foreigners'. It was here the little dark people from the Mediterranean landed in the Megalithic days to set up their great stone circles and long forgotten burial mounds.

They were dark secretive men, these Cornish ancestors, spending most of the day down gloomy tin mines and even when they saw 'down cloudy cliffs through sheets of foam' the Phoenician merchants and other 'shy traffickers' approaching the beach to 'undo their corded bales', the canny old Cornish tribes chased them over to the quays on St. Michael's Mount to unload, rather than have 'foreigners' loose upon the mainland.

So what greater variety could any cruising ground offer you, with good harbours and pleasant pubs thrown in, when you eventually make your chosen port after the day's sail. Like the Sultan's ring, you can have the best of both worlds, the excitement of rocky shores and the pleasant sense of achievement at the day's end. You will remember, the Sultan was given a new magnificent ring and he asked his Grand Vizier to devise an engraving of no more than six words for it which would both help him in adversity and keep him modest in prosperity. The Grand Vizier wrote,

'And this also, shall pass away.'

What a comforting motto to have in the cockpit on one of those particularly unpleasant cold, rough night passages that crop up every now and then in spite of the weatherman's bland assurances.

Lyme Bay

Anyway, enough of idle thoughts; we are on our way west, across Lyme Bay, which, to the yachtsman, is a kind of no man's land separating the delights of the Solent from the anticipation of winding Devon rivers and picturesque old Cornish harbours. There are no navigational dangers; even Portland Bill which forms the eastern boundary to the Bay is safe enough provided you go well outside the Race or are sufficiently familiar with the area to take the inside passage between it and the Bill and manage to dodge the lobster pots in places where loss of control might have unpleasant results. If you are in a hurry and the wind is favourable, you can of course forget the Dorset harbours and run direct across the forty miles or so from Portland Bill to Hope's Nose or Berry Head, but on a leisurely cruising holiday this may be a longer passage than many like to make in a small boat and it would be a great pity to ignore the little Dorset harbours if the weather is fine and the wind offshore.

Sailing across Lyme Bay can be a bit of a dreary flog, because to appreciate the view you really have to approach it from much further out to sea – perhaps on passage from the Channel Islands or the Cotentin Peninsular. Golden Cap will appear first as a smudge on the horizon, but on a clear day the whole sweep of this bay will gradually emerge, rather as the peaks emerge during a dawn climb of a Swiss mountain and, lit by an afternoon sun they are visible from thirty or forty miles away. Seen from that distance it has a quite unforgettable beauty of outline, though you may be too far away to distinguish the variety of colourings which are one of the main joys of this coastline.

Bridport

So we will close the coast and make for Bridport at the western end of the Chesil Beach in case a word or two about it will help you if you decide to follow suit. And don't be put off by our old friend Frank Cowper when he says in 1909,

> 'A friend of mine, who used to yacht a great deal, gave it as his opinion that Bridport was "a beastly place," as none but coasters frequent it. I can fully endorse this view. But Lyme, to my mind, is much worse. There is no safety even in it, and an old Coastguard officer, who remembered the days of Marryat, told me that in those days the Coastguard cutter which used to be here was built nearly solid to stand the bumping she got inside the Cobb.'

He was obviously not attending to his weather and got caught by an onshore wind, in which case these ports are not tenable. You have only to look at the photograph opposite page 16 which I took on our last visit when there was a mere Force 5 gusting to 6, to appreciate the point.

This is because West Bay, or Bridport Haven as it is called, faces the prevailing wind in the widest part of the Channel. Not until one reaches Mount's Bay in Cornwall, where the prevailing sou'westers roll in straight from the Atlantic, is there a more exposed spot. There is a long narrow entrance to what is really an artificial harbour and the entrance practically dries out at L.W.S.

There are no offshore dangers and as long as you don't mind taking the ground or lying against the quay in soft mud I still think it is well worth a visit. You risk a sudden change of wind which might mean an enforced wait in port – but no more than other West Country harbours.

It must have been a fearsome place to get into in the days of pure sail as ships would have had to warp in under most conditions. But at every harbour in the world there always seems to be a group of men standing about watching the ships and I expect Bridport was no exception. They would all be expected to lend a hand.

West Bay, as you will find, is a pleasant little port, with some old cottages and the pub where Charles II waited for a boat for France when escaping after the battle of Worcester. Otherwise there is little excitement and the town of Bridport, an old 'rope town' filling the gap between green hills, is two miles away.

Lyme Regis

If the weather holds and the wind still has no south in it Lyme Regis with its famous Cobb, one of the oldest piers in England, is very visitable. It is a pleasant town with good inns but, I am afraid a not very comfortable harbour unless you have legs or at least twin keels, because it has silted up and the bottom is a bit hard to sit on comfortably.

The Cobb, Lyme Regis.

Despite the discomforts, Lyme at one time was a considerable trading port, even importing such valuable products as gold dust and ivory from Africa in addition to its rather closer ties with Morlaix in Brittany. By the nineteenth century cargoes were perhaps a little more ordinary but in 1879 they were still extensive enough for the Cobb Clerk, W.J. Atkins, to post a tariff which is still there for a wide range of merchandise including stores, timber, slate, barrels and bottles. A few items from this tariff taken at random read:-

'For every empty barrell	1d
For every truss of sailcloth	6d
For every coach or four wheeled vehicle	2s.0
For every ton of butter or cheese	1s.0'

I certainly remember coal boats still using this harbour as late as the 1930's, though they couldn't get in at low water.

So, if the weather is right and you are prepared to dry out against the quay there is no reason why you should not go into Lyme and wallow in its history. You can read about its part in the Civil War, the Monmouth rebellion and Jane Austen in any guide book but if you want to be 'with it' now-a-days, you hunt for fossils along the beach and in the cliffs. It is only 160 years ago that Mary Anning, the ten year old daughter of an old curiosity shop keeper found the remains – all twenty-five feet of them – of the *Ichthyosaurus Platydon.* He is now cosily tucked up in the South Kensington Natural History Museum.

More fun perhaps is to walk through the famous Landslip between Lyme and Seaton, which used to be one of our favourite places when we stayed here as children. Despite the good footpath there was always a feeling of adventure and exploration as we followed the narrow track, which twisted and turned through the lush undergrowth and over the crisp springy turf of steep little hillocks. Half way along, there used to be an old cottage which was said to have come down bodily with the cliff and remained intact. Fortunately this didn't seem to have affected the production of wonderful cream teas which always added wings to our little feet as we made for the wooden benches in the old orchard.

With an offshore wind you could spend a very happy few days here, even perhaps anchored outside the harbour in preference to taking the ground inside. But I am afraid you should never look on either Lyme or Bridport as ports of refuge; they are fair weather stops only.

From Lyme Regis to Exmouth

Soon we shall be getting a little shelter from the sou'westerlies because after Exmouth the mainland runs practically north and south, until Start Point is reached. This means that entering or leaving port can be more often when it suits us rather than the weather. You can keep about half a mile offshore, because there are no dangers except at the river mouths and headlands, until we get to Hope's Nose off Torquay. The first day's sail is an easy twenty miles into the Exe which is well worth a day or two before making for Torbay.

Though there is no usable harbour before Exmouth the coast from Lyme Regis is full of interest, and you can enjoy the pleasant red and white cliffs with their bright green grassy caps and the variety of the hills and valleys of the hinterland.

On the far side of Haven Point you will find a long stretch of steep-to shingle banks with no apparent way through, unless you spot a small stream coming out on the eastern side. If it happens to be near high water you may indeed see a small dinghy or motor boat coming out. This is an interesting little survival because it is really the entrance to the old harbour of Axmouth Haven, about which Leland wrote in the sixteenth century:-

> 'Ther hath been a very notable haven at Seaton, but now there lyith between the two points of the old haven a mighty rigge and barre of pible stones in the very mouth of it, and the river Axe is driven to the very Est point of the haven Caullid Whitclif, and ther at a very small gut goith into the sea; and ther come in small fisschar boats for soccur.'

Later the whole entrance was blocked and not until last century, when some local farmers made an abortive attempt to open it again,

Bridport – not to be recommended in on-shore winds.

The small drying-out harbour at Lyme Regis.

At Beer the fishing boats are just pulled up on the beach.

Exeter – the Maritime Museum is near the centre of the town. (Photo by courtesy of the I.S.C.A.)

was anything done about it. But this modern pressure in the twentieth century for somewhere to keep a boat has revived the efforts and now the locals have patched up quite a cosy little home at the back for a dozen or so small boats. There is still very little water, not more than a foot or two I would guess over the bar but it's rather fun to find an old port beginning to come back into use again.

Guillemot – a few words from Father!

Seaton itself is not a particularly attractive seaside resort but a little further on you come to the charming little fishing village of Beer, which is really just a pebble beach at the end of a narrow valley between two great chalk cliffs. There is no pretence at all of any sort of a harbour and the fishing boats are launched on rollers over the shingle. But there it is, still a fishing village of some consequence and if the weather is really calm you can anchor off and go in by dinghy for lunch or at least a noggin at either of the two pleasant inns. You will find a few yachts pulled up on the beach with the fishing boats; but you will notice they are not using any of the few buoys offshore which is a sure enough indication that whatever the Pilot books say about the delights of Beer as an anchorage in northerly winds I would not leave our own yacht there very long, as

I have a suspicion the holding ground is not at all good.

Apart from its undoubted charm, the little village of Beer is really only noted for two things, smuggling and the more legitimate industry of lace making. In the latter it has the unique distinction of having made Queen Victoria's wedding dress. Its reputation for smuggling, piracy and privateering is of course shared by every harbour on this coast, and, indeed, an old chronical I remember sets down that the men of Beer,

> 'Lusted exceedingly after the blood and treasure of
> the French Corsairs and other sea rovers.'

Not only was fishing a secondary occupation for many but for long periods piracy was given a Royal cloak of respectability and called privateering. Indeed, according to the *Libel of English Policy* Edward III

> 'did Dewise of English towns three, that is to say,
> Dartmouth Plymouth and the third it is Fowey; and
> gave them help and puissance upon pety Britayne
> for to werre.'

Sometimes the chaps worked independently but now and then combined into quite sizeable expeditions and carried on a pleasantly profitable private war, as when in the fourteenth century the men of Dartmouth collected their allies, the men of Portsmouth and sailed into the Seine where they sank four French ships, captured four others, including the barge of De Clisson 'stored with splendid booty', as a contemporary chronicler puts it.

The River Exe

Exmouth

Coming from the east, Exmouth itself is not too difficult to find as the entrance is well buoyed and parallel to the shore after rounding Straight Point, about half a mile offshore at the seaward end. If you are coming from the west, however, it is a little more difficult because, as you will see from your chart, you have to keep nearly a mile offshore to avoid the Pole Sands and find the Fairway buoy, which for some reason is always a bit difficult to spot. There is a short cut called the Western Way but I would not advise this if you are coming in for the first time or unless you see a boat with your own draught going in ahead of you. As to entrance at night there are actually leading lights so I suppose it is theoretically possible to get in but I have never done it and I must admit I wouldn't care to try. Near the town, there is not too much room to anchor and stay afloat and in many places the tide runs too fast for safety so I would suggest you find the Harbour Master and see if he can fit you into the dock or find you a mooring.

The Exeter Canal

Except at the height of the season there is usually room to anchor up river between Warren Point and Starcross, or you may like to run up on the tide to Topsham and dry out against the quay for a pleasant evening in this old town which was once the port for Exeter. Indeed I am told that as late as William III's reign Topsham's trade with Newfoundland was more extensive than that of any other port except London.

Another possibility is to anchor near the entrance to the canal where you will find very good snacks at the *Turf Inn,* but I do really hope, if you have a day to spare or have the bad luck to be gale bound in Exmouth, that you follow the coasters up river through the canal to Exeter where there is any amount of fun to be had apart from the old town itself. I should perhaps begin by giving you one word of warning before you try the canal for the five miles to Exeter. There is sometimes a delay and it would be a seamanlike precaution to phone in advance to the Canal Foreman (Exeter 71910). Having made arrangements, there is no problem. There are double locks in the middle and a *Double Locks Hotel,* where again you can get at least jolly good snacks and beer at most times of the season. They don't do full meals as far as I remember.

Perhaps a short word as to the history might make the trip a little more fun for you. Until the late thirteenth century small craft were able to come up to the town by the watergate but during the reign of Edward I the river was blocked by the building of a weir. Nothing was done for some time until the present canal was started in 1564. After that, ships of sixteen tons could go up to Exeter through the three pound locks, which are interesting as they are the earliest pound locks in the country. In 1825 the canal was extended for a further two miles to Turf and widened so that craft of 400 tons and drawing fourteen feet could get up to Exeter. Nowadays the commercial traffic has declined and may indeed stop altogether as soon as the motorway is driven across it but it is increasingly used by yachts.

Exeter

Once up in Exeter itself there are splendid quays against which to lie, the whole of the town quay or the quay on the museum side. Mr. Thomas, the harbour master will make you very welcome and find you a good place where you won't be disturbed. The quay is very convenient for the Cathedral and the interesting parts of the town, apart from which and possibly of more immediate interest, there is the *Port Royal Inn* below the quay and the *Prospect Inn* just above, also the fishmarket and the customs house. The Maritime Museum is in itself a most interesting place and well worth a visit. They have an extraordinary range of boats from pearling dhows and jalibots of Bahrein to a reed boat from Lake Titicaca, Doctor and Mrs Pye's *Moonraker of Fowey* an ex Looe fishing lugger built in 1896, a Fijian proa, a British Channel pilot cutter and a delightful old steam tug *St Canute* built in Denmark in 1931, not to mention Welsh corracles, curraghs from County Kerry and the Bedford lifeboat built in 1886. Some of these, including a state barge, are still afloat and can be inspected.

Thoughts on How the Coast was Formed

While we are resting quietly in port may I put another thought into your mind. Just as I suggested in *The Solent from the Sea* that you would find pleasure in looking up something about the birds, let me suggest another hobby which could similarly increase the interest of a cruise. In coastal cruising you are always looking at the scenery – have you ever wondered how it was put together? Even while you are beginning to read up a few elementary facts you can be doing amateur detective stuff and diagnosing the age and order of rock formations, and you will soon find yourself getting quite excited about deciding how this or that type of landscape was put together. If not of course you can skip the next page or so!

There is, however, no better place to start than from a boat, for the cliff face is in reality a clean slice down through geological history because the action of the sea cuts a straight section through the cliffs rather like a knife cutting a slice of rich cake to reveal the goodies within.

It can be said that a piece of scenery is pleasant to the eye or ugly or to some it may be just a jumble of hills and valleys that have no meaning. Now all I am suggesting is that, without spending a lot of time studying geology seriously, you can easily pick up enough facts to begin to see that the scenic features have a plan and a system underlying their layout. Once this is understood the landscape begins to fall into place and the form and variety assumes a new and lively interest for the viewer. After all you are only trying to do for yourself what any artist or poet does when he attempts to give a little humanly understandable form to the natural processes he is observing and, to my mind, there is one great advantage in this sort of interpretation, you can begin to have your fun almost before you start acquiring the knowledge to understand the processes involved. You don't need the literary ability of the poet or the manual skill of the artist because the study of scenery is essentially a layman's hobby and from the first the beginner has the opportunity to make original observations, to weigh up the evidence he sees with his own eyes and to make deductions from the facts as he comes across them. Who knows, he may even get interested enough to want to know more, so that he can make even better deductions and I have provided for this possibility by suggesting a few pleasant elementary books in the bibliography that you may wish to take with you on your cruise. It is no fun taking other people's ready made conclusions and this field is wide open; why not have a tentative shot at making your own?

Cormorant drying wings.

Now this is no place to try to condense a large technical volume to a few paragraphs – even if I had the ability to do so. But I will try and pick out a few simple basic essentials so that you can make a start on the scenery of this stretch of coast.

You will probably remember that once the earth had cooled sufficiently for the original old rocks to solidify into a crust about forty miles thick, all sorts of exiciting things began to happen during the last four thousand million years. Geologists tend to be a bit vague

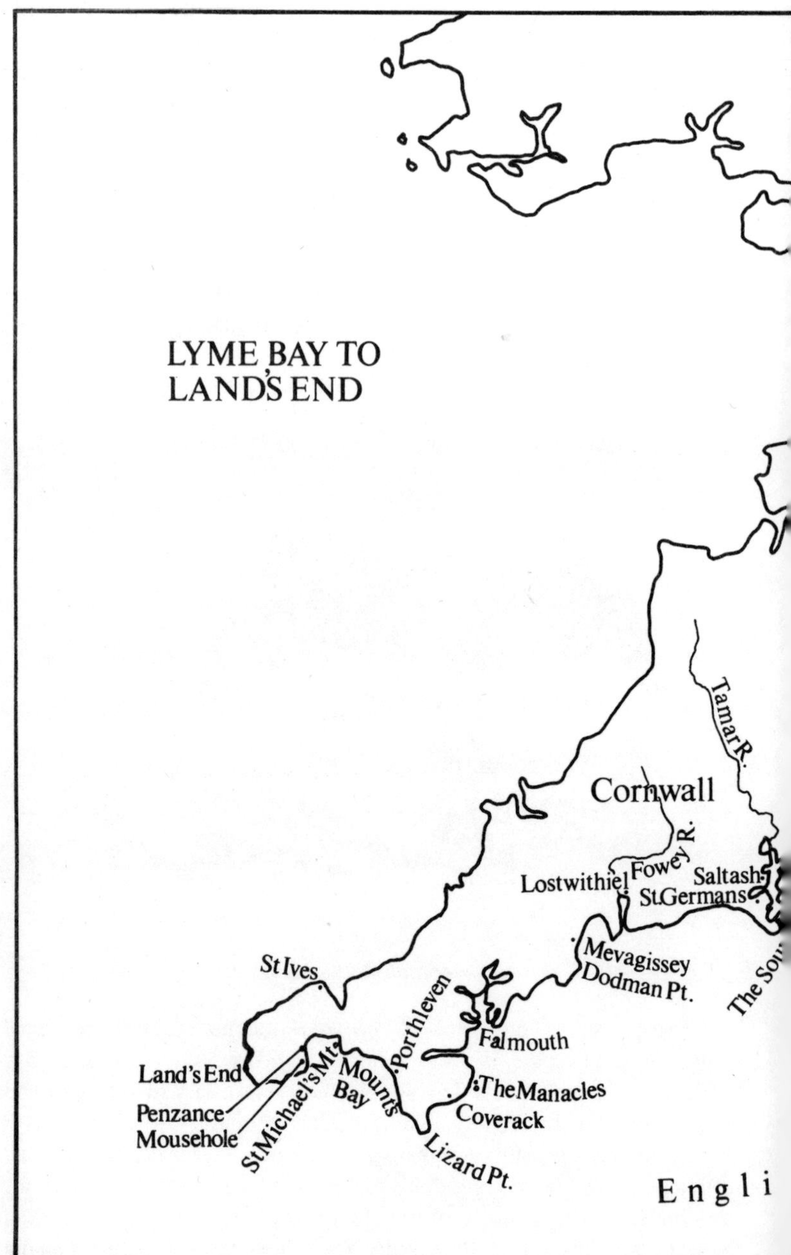
LYME BAY TO
LAND'S END
Cornwall
Tamar R.
Fowey R.
Lostwithiel
Saltash
St.Germans
Mevagissey
Dodman Pt.
The Sou
St Ives
Porthleven
Falmouth
Land's End
Penzance
Mousehole
St Michael's Mt.
Mounts Bay
The Manacles
Coverack
Lizard Pt.
Engli

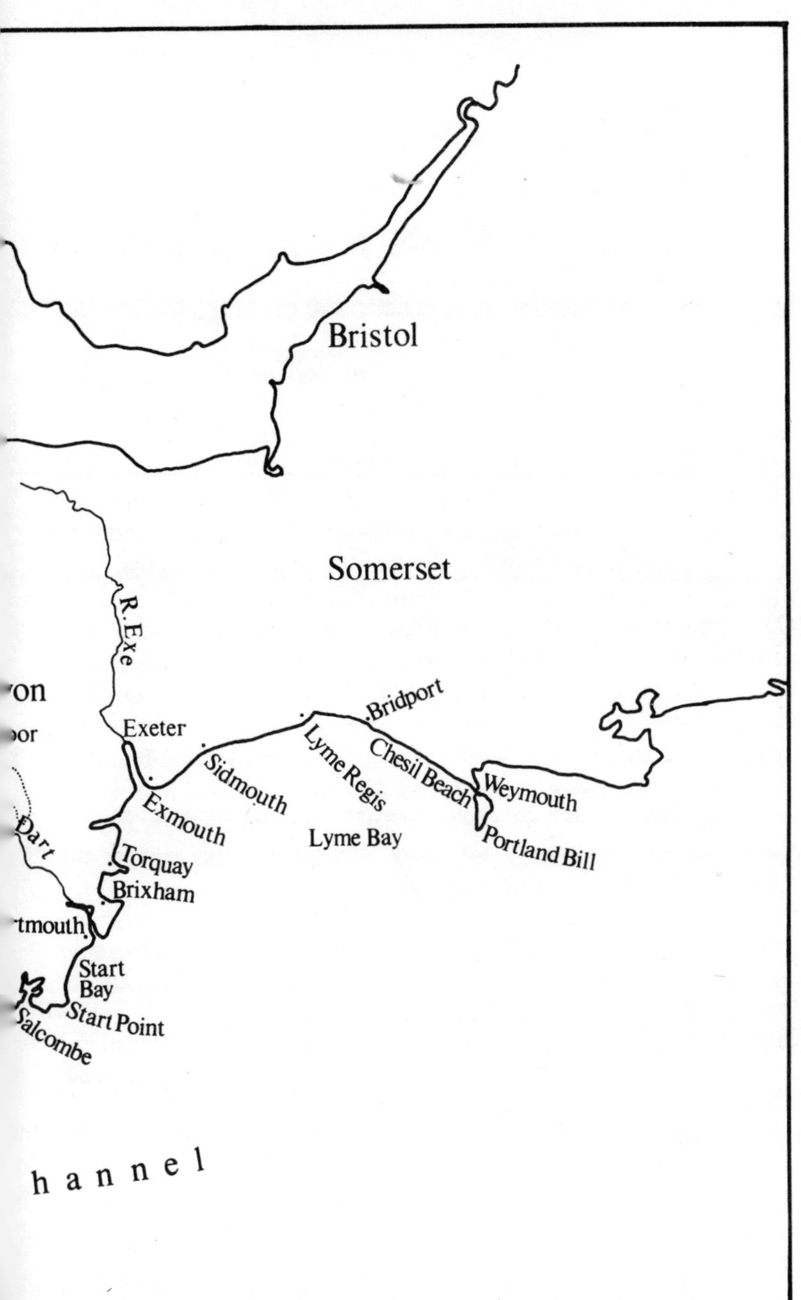
Bristol
Somerset
R. Exe
Exeter
Exmouth
Sidmouth
Lyme Regis
Bridport
Chesil Beach
Weymouth
Portland Bill
Lyme Bay
Dart
Torquay
Brixham
Start
Bay
Start Point
Salcombe

still about the first two thousand million years but knowledge of the period after that is accumulating fast with modern methods of identification.

Types of Rocks

To begin with I should merely divide the rocks that you see into three main types:-

(1) Igneous, or fire formed rocks like basalt or the granite you find on the Tors of Dartmoor and at other places along the coast, particularly Land's End. These rocks are still being thrown up by volcanoes in various parts of the world or forced into rifts, often in the ocean bed where whole continents have drifted about and forced pressurised cracks in the surface of the crust by squeezing land masses together or pulling them apart. For instance, we now know that North and South America broke away from Africa to form the Atlantic and Greenland was once joined to Scotland as the rocks show.

(2) Sedimentary rocks like sandstone or shale which are really fine particles of old rocks broken down by rain, frost and wind, then carted away to sea by rivers and glaciers. These are then deposited on the sea bed like layers of a fancy cake and either forced up above the surface again by pressure or left high and dry by a general raising of the land surface above the sea level. If you think back to Bridport which we have just left or any other cliffs you know well, which are formed of horizontal layers of rocks often of different colours and texture, you will see the process at its simplest. There are also the non crystalline limestones and softer chalk which was originally formed under the water by accumulation of countless millions of shell fish and sea creatures called *foraminifera.* The white cliffs of Dover, the Seven Sisters at Beachy Head, the Needles and the cliffs above them on the Isle of Wight are the best known examples of the chalk cliffs of our South coast. You will also remember the chalk headland at Beer Head; going west that is the last you will see of the chalk which disappears.

(3) Lastly there are a whole range of what are called metamorphic rocks like marble, crystalline limestones and slate which are older rocks which have been changed into new types by the action of heat, pressure or chemical agents.

Types of Countryside

Now each of these types of rock gives us a distinctive type of countryside which you can quite quickly get to recognise in spite of the superficial layer of soil and other organic matter brought about by the woods and vegetation which now covers it. The old cottages will also tell you a lot about the rocks because they tend to be built of local materials whereas churches were often built of foreign stone transported for effect. Along this coast we first had the smooth contoured round hills of the Dorset chalk country behind Bridport and soon we shall be into the older world of the bleak granite moorlands of Devon and the craggy volcanic cliffs of the Cornish coast like the serpentine cliffs above Mullion Cove. There are no spectacular high moors as in the North but the southern coastal plain has a wonderful variety of rocks because of the mixture of slates and sandstones intermingled with massive limestone and volcanic rocks.

This leads to a very irregular coastline because the resistance to the battering it gets from the sea waves varies according to the toughness of the cliff rocks. This is especially noticeable round Torquay where there are bold headlands, dainty bays and a wonderful contrast in colours. And another example, you may remember as we turned west from Lyme we were immediately confronted with one of the possible effects of sea action undermining the whole cliff by working away at its base. Where the cliff is formed of different layers of rocks and particularly if one of them is good slippery clay it cannot survive indefinitely the destruction of its foundations and a collapse is inevitable. This is what happened on that Christmas night in 1839 when some eight million tons of earth came down. I hope you may have had time to walk along there yesterday and see how completely nature has managed to cover up the scars, while today from the sea you are in the best position to appreciate the magnitude of the slip. It is worth having a good look at the cliffs of Oddicombe as you go by and see if you can spot how this has been cut back by wave action between projecting cliffs of limestone along a belt of new red sandstone which has been super-imposed along the line of an old fault in the older rocks. You see a similar type of scenery in the cliffs of Teignmouth and Dawlish.

A little further on you will see why the headland ending in Hope's Nose has resisted all attempts to wash it away – it is backed by the hard igneous rocks of Black Head. Hope's Nose is again fairly hard limestone, like most of the other projecting headlands further on and this has resisted erosion, while the softer slates and sandstones have been carved away into little coves and small bays. The shapes of the bays often depend on the angle of the layers of sandstone and where they have been pressure folded into great curves. The weathering has followed the line and developed beautiful curves in the resultant natural scenery.

There is such a wealth of interesting, I would say exciting, geological happenings that have gone to make up the varied scenery of this delightful bit of coast that I have no time even to bring to your attention because the publishers have very definite ideas about the length of book they want. So I will take just one more example of the sort of detective fun you can have and this time we will take a cut, not along the coast, but at right angles up into the countryside – in fact up the Dart estuary that you will be visiting shortly to enjoy its wonderful crags and subsidiary creeks.

Like the Fal it is an old valley that was drowned by subsidence of the land during Neolithic times. Before this it must have been a quite remarkable steep sided gorge. Even now it is particularly exciting because the river cuts through rocks of several different types which are easily distinguishable. If you use the tide to do the bit between Dittisham and Totnes you will find a series of volcanic lavas and other igneous rocks which are excellent examples of how Devon itself was formed about 320 million years ago. They are directly responsible for the rugged beauty of the Dart estuary and the woods that have grown up on the rock formations have completed the picture.

At the same time you can see how the softer sedimentary rocks have given us a quite different type of scenery along the small tributary rivers with the softer gentler slopes of the valleys because the underlying rocky structure has been worn down and smoothed over much more easily by wind, frost and rain – Old Mill Creek is a good example. Also, opposite Dittisham itself you will see how the river has been able to widen out quite exceptionally because it is running through an area of soft slate.

Well, so it goes on, and you can work out each estuary for yourself as you potter up to the local pub for the evening's drink.

From Exmouth to Teignmouth

We must move on out of the Exe and have a look at Teignmouth. For no very logical reason it is along this part of the coast that one first begins to realise one has arrived in the land of pixies and fairies and those rather pleasant pockets where the Celtic legends still linger in spite of an Anglo Saxon population with a twentieth century mania for illogical local government amenity statistics. Indeed, was not Exeter itself the acknowledged head-quarters of witchcraft. The great White Witch of that city was the local Queen Bee of all witches. Being a witch might have been chancy at times. I mean there were no half measures; you either scared the pants off the neighbours or you came rapidly to a sticky end. I have a shrewed notion that like the 'Scotsman' stories, the legends of witches and warlocks were put about and sustained mostly by the witches themselves because it was good for trade.

After all, I should know, after serving for many years in the R.A.F. abroad between the wars. One of my bearers who could see further round corners than most folk can achieve in a straight line always claimed solemnly that his mother had become pregnant by a dragon – well, they say, only the woman really knows.

And there was the time in West Africa when I spent three days as a Witch Doctor's assistant. We really had a bit of a problem on our hands because, in addition to intensive staging post activities, we were trembling on the brink of an A.O.C's inspection and suddenly one fine morning all the local tribal maintenance staff from the hangers disappeared into the hills and work over the whole aerodrome came to a grinding halt. The head man explained through a local Flight Sergeant that a 'hoodoo' had been placed on the hangars and sleeping quarters. The Adjutant thought this was a bit uncivil and we agreed with him but the head man was adamant – only a qualified witch doctor who knew the drill could lift it. Well, 'Would he get hold of one!' Yes, he thought that could be arranged – at a price. They were all, apparently very busy at that time and that meant inflation, but he agreed to see what he could do. It would be a three day job anyway, we learned.

The raising of the hoodoo was solemnly put out to tender and when these were received, even the lowest was far above the slender potentialities of available funds and it was felt that reference to F.11 in the Air Ministry for supplementary funds for reimbursement of local witch doctor was unlikely to be favourably received. We were truly in the gummy. The local tribes were polite but firm; they would carry out their normal duties in the most punctilious and airmanlike manner but *not* in the vicinity of the hangers or sleeping quarters until! I must admit to having a certain sympathy with the witch doctors. It is after all an old and venerated profession and generally handed down traditionally from father to son in normal circumstances. Now and then an outsider tries to break in but it is an expensive occupation. There is the salary, to start with, of an assistant to be considered – vital for the placing of money under remote stones in the forest so that after due incantation it can be prophesied to be there and subsequently, to the astonishment of the tribesmen, actually found after the spirits have dictated the route to be followed.

Anyway, at the eleventh hour, the breakthrough! It came to light that in the case of a mere hoodoo *removal* honour would be served if the ritual – all three days of it – were to be performed by an assistant working under the instructions of a qualified witch doctor. Needless to say, the Adjutant and I put ourselves under instruction and, on the appointed day, in the presence of some three thousand tribal maintenance aircraftsmen we solemnly went through the daily ritual of incantations with little ceremonial fires. We even burnt rather revolting bits of dead animals till – voilà, no more hoodoo and all the levies trooped happily back to work and to their sleeping quarters, just in time for the annual inspection.

Whew – but the Adjutant's report to Group Headquarters and thence to Command and Air Ministry, though a gem of official language was, I'm afraid received and duly initialled with a certain air of scepticism together with my own very modest request for extra duty pay as 'assistant witch doctor extraordinary'. I only mention this to explain why, though not claiming to be in quite the same social strata as the most distinguished witches and warlocks to be found in Devon and Cornwall, I can claim a certain sympathetic understanding of their problems and of the importance of their place in the life and thought of the West Country. There are very few stretches of this coast without visual evidence of their past activities.

For instance just on this bit of the coast a jutting crag on Hole Head just north of Teignmouth, our next port of call, is really all that remains of the rapacious local parson after, in this case the Devil rather than the witches had done with him and just offshore, frozen for ever in rock like form, is his clerk. Any local will tell you the sad story. Apparently quite a lot of the God men had been having a bean feast in Exeter, mostly to try and get themselves elected as Bishop because the old man had just died. On the way home the weather really clamped down and this particular parson with his clerk got lost in the trackless moors on their way back to Teignmouth. The clerk's writing was obviously better than his sense of direction because they were soon well and truly lost and the infuriated parson got very cross and incautiously shouted, 'I would rather have the Devil for a guide than you!' Well, you know as well as I do that this was a tricky thing to say in the eighteenth century because you were apt to be taken at your word, sometimes inconveniently! Not long afterwards a local rode up, whom they hadn't noticed until that moment, and volunteered to lead them to shelter. The offer was of course eagerly accepted and before long the guide brought them to a lonely house where all the windows were brightly lit and there was obviously a whale of a party going on inside. Wild choruses could be heard coming out of the windows but by this time both master and man were only too glad to be under cover and far too tired and cross to be critical of the entertainment. They were soon at supper with companions who might have caused them a little uneasiness had they been less tired. It wasn't until they were both feeling, well, 'very nicely thank you' that the parson's little conscience began to stir and he demanded a guide so that they could continue their journey. The whole party came to the front door to see them off but the next snag was that no sooner were they mounted than they found the horses wouldn't move. The priest beat them with his whip to no effect and the house party all cheered and then he seems to have blotted his copybook for the second time, 'The Devil's in the horses', he cried, 'But Devil or no Devil they shall go.' Whereupon there was a roar of approval from the house guests; the house vanished and the company, which had unaccountably all grown forked tails, capered with glee. The waters of the sea rose round the two wretched men now clinging to the flanks of their horses for dear life while a flash of lightning showed up their guide tail and all.

Eventually in the morning the parson was found turned into a nice solid bit of granite on the cliff while away out to sea was his clerk who – as you can see – is still there. Nothing much seems to have happened to the horses which, being sensible animals, went quietly home, none the worse for their night's adventure.

Teignmouth

Teignmouth, now full on the starboard bow, has again I'm afraid a very tricky changing entrance, and is not as well buoyed as Exmouth. It has of course been sacked once or twice by the French, not to mention one or two occasions when the fleet of fishing boats was seized. In between these normal excitements and in spite of its awkward and shallow entrance, it became and is still quite a busy little port, its trade varying over the centuries from fishing, fish curing and salt making to china clay which was brought down from Newton Abbot in barges and exchanged for wood pulp and timber from Norway. If you go in you will find it an attractive little town which nestles nicely under its cliff but I am afraid at the risk of suffering the local wrath I can really only advise it for another quick visit. Apart from the entrance, there is not really very much room to anchor inside because The Salty, which dries out, occupies most of the space and a strong tidal stream and a fair number of coasters don't really make for yachtsmen's comfort. If you have, on the other hand, a small motor boat and can run under the bridge it becomes a different matter because the upper river is well worth exploring by dinghy. Also if you have legs you have a slightly wider choice of berth but I think your best bet as usual is to try the harbour master and he can often fit you in somewhere.

The Brixham fishing fleet in port.

The 'Royal Castle Hotel', Dartmouth.

The Dart – looking north from Dittisham.

The Salcombe entrance on a stormy day.

Torbay

On the passage across Babbacombe Bay you can see that the red cliffs we are by now so accustomed to are giving place to grey rocks which first appear to the north of Oddicombe Beach. The Beach itself is of the now familiar new red sandstone but to the south as well as to the north, it is bordered by these great grey cliffs of Devonian limestone, a considerably older rock than the sandstone. Oddicombe Beach is a nice example of the way in which a fault in the older rocks gets filled up with a later layer of sedimentary rocks to give these pleasant variegated effects.

From here to Berry Head on the far side of Brixham you will notice that all the headlands except one (Black Head which is a bit of a freak) are formed of this attractive limestone which, being as you remember soluble, makes for interesting caves in the cliffs. Despite this, it is much more resistant to wave action than the sandstones, whether red, yellow or grey, and so we get the bays and coves which are such a delightful feature of this bit of coast. Above Hope's Nose the sea has carved out two of the loveliest bays, Babbacombe and Anstey's and so long as there is no east in the wind you can anchor in these in reasonable safety. As popular beauty spots they may get a bit crowded during the day but you will have the beaches to yourself at night. Once round Hope's Nose into Torbay itself you will see the results of the sea action on a much grander scale, for the two great limestone headlands Hope's Nose and Berry Head are more than four miles apart and the bay which has formed between them is over two and a half miles wide. You will also notice, incidentally, that outlying rocks are beginning to appear round the headlands, necessitating a wider berth. Some of them, like the Ore Stone off Hope's Nose and the various Mewstones at the entrance to several rivers, are like miniature islands; others are so small that when the sea is choppy you need a good lookout if you are prone to short cuts. I know most of the rocks are steep to and if you like that sort of thing you can sail quite close and look down at them through the clear water, but unless you really know the area well or the pilot guides recommend a particular passage, I would resist the temptation to take too many short cuts between the rocks and the shore.

The northern end of Torbay is one of the few places where there is a safe short cut, passage between Ore Stone and the Point. Once in the bay, you are in safe water with a choice of three harbours and a possible anchorage offshore unless the wind is in the east. This is now such a popular holiday area that one forgets its prosperity is only two hundred years old. In the Middle Ages Tor Abbey with its broad acres and money pouring in from the woollen industry, was the only prosperous establishment. The rest of the district consisted of little fishing hamlets – you have only to look at the buildings to see a splendid display of Victoriana. The difficulty was that, sheltered as the whole bay is from the prevailing winds, it has no natural harbours and, even more important, no harbours with entrances narrow enough to be defensible in the days of pirates and privateers. The bay was a well known anchorage especially during the Napoleonic Wars but, before that, it was equally well patronised by the French when the English fleet was away attending to the Dutch or simply resting through shortage of money and Royal support. It was from here in 1690 that the French sent their galleys with 1,700 men to attack and burn Teignmouth.

Torquay

The transformation of Torquay from a fishing village to a great holiday resort seems to have been due initially to two things. First, the growth of trade in the latter half of the eighteenth century, particularly with Newfoundland, began to bring more shipping to its good, long quay. Secondly, as I have already said, the fleet was beginning to use the bay during the Napoleonic wars and the officers with their families needed houses – the result was the development of the Strand as it is still called today. Thus the town was already growing rapidly when, at the beginning of the next century, Sir Lawrence Palk started to construct the harbour, especially the part which today is known as the Inner Basin. With the later addition of

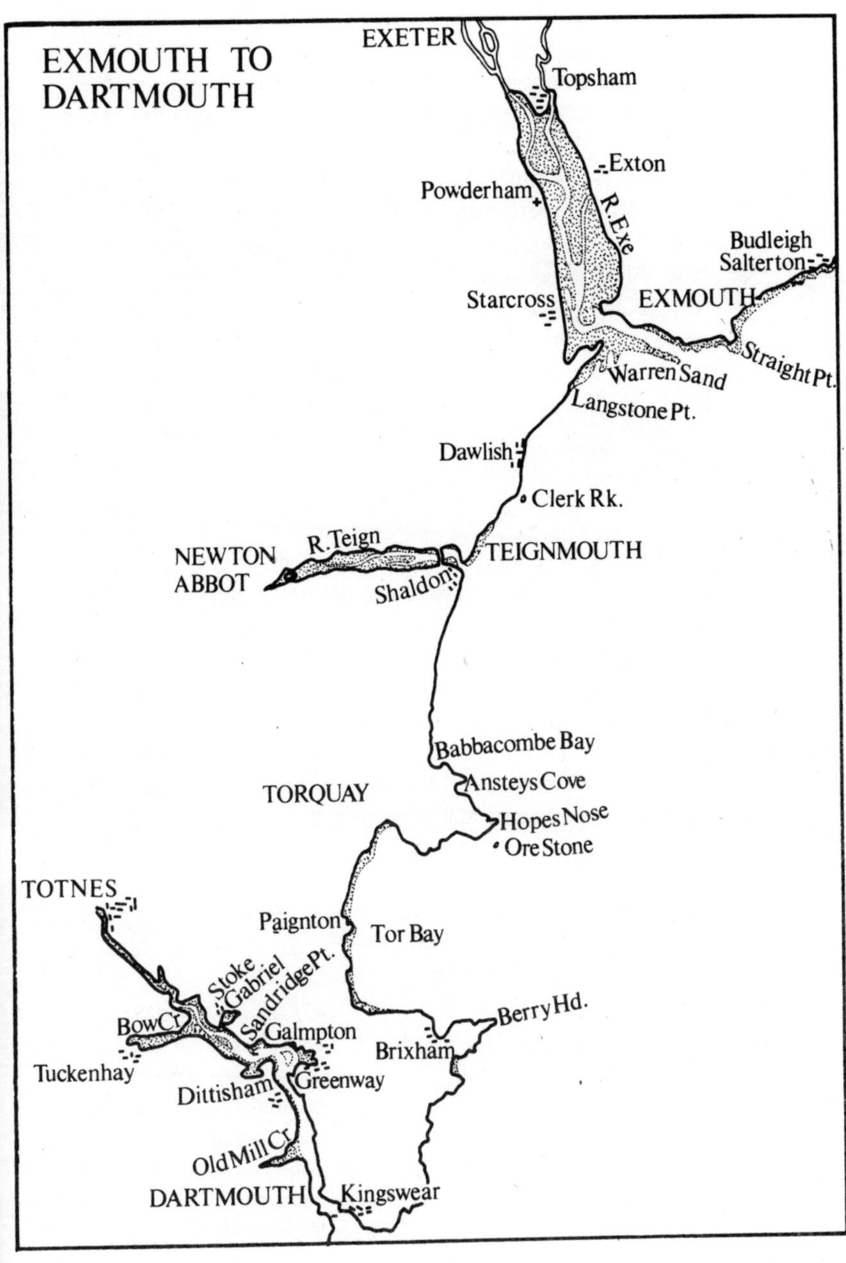
EXMOUTH TO
DARTMOUTH
EXETER
Topsham
Exton
Powderham
R.Exe
Budleigh
Salterton
Starcross
EXMOUTH
Straight Pt.
Warren Sand
Langstone Pt.
Dawlish
Clerk Rk.
R.Teign
NEWTON
ABBOT
TEIGNMOUTH
Shaldon
Babbacombe Bay
Ansteys Cove
TORQUAY
Hopes Nose
Ore Stone
TOTNES
Paignton
Tor Bay
Stoke
Gabriel
Sandridge Pt.
Bow Cr.
Galmpton
Berry Hd.
Brixham
Tuckenhay
Dittisham
Greenway
Old Mill Cr.
DARTMOUTH
Kingswear

the much larger outer harbour, the future of Tor Key as it was by this time being called, was assured. The modern harbour is popular – with excursion boats as well as yachts – but it is inevitably crowded and in a south east wind uncomfortable owing to the scend in the outer harbour, while the Inner Harbour dries out and is only used by dinghies. If you like this sort of place, and please don't let me put you off, the harbour master will fit you in somewhere if he can. I must admit we find Brixham much cosier and full of jolly pubs and fishing boats.

You could look in at Paignton on the way, but it is really too small for comfort and dries out completely. You may get a Chess Congress (September) thrown in for good measure. But I think Brixham is by far the more attractive place with its steep hills and terraces of old houses over-looking the harbour.

Brixham

It still has a considerable fishing fleet which has for years claimed to catch the best fish along the coast and though you can stock up with freshly caught fish for breakfast, I should keep clear of the fairway when the fishing fleet roars in late on the tide so that they can unload at the fish market. Elsewhere, yachts may have to share a harbour uncomfortably with the fisherman, but here you can anchor or ask for a yacht club mooring in the roomy outer harbour – and you will find the yacht club officials most helpful. With its long breakwater it is well sheltered and there is good landing at all stages of the tide. So long as you are well clear of the fairway – and the wash from excursion boats – you will be peaceful enough but if you want something even quieter and the wind is not in the north you might try Elbury or Churston Coves – with a good golf course on your doorstep if you are that way inclined.

In passing, there are two events in English history to which Devon claims a proprietory right, the Armada and the landing of William of Orange. The former I think we should leave until we get around to Plymouth but the latter belongs indisputably to Brixham. And with his statue dominating the harbour we had better give him at least a mention – unattractive old dumpling though he was. While James II was waiting comfortably for an invasion up the Thames the Dutch fleet had slipped down the Channel with what his adversaries called 'a Protestant wind' and on the morning of the 5th November 1688 anchored off Brixham.

It was a misty morning and the population, when they awoke, must have been a bit foxed by a large number of odd shaped boats, as they dimly made them out emerging from the mist. Even when the sun rose and the crowds, which had by this time gathered on the

The fish market, Brixham.

cliffs could see clearly, there was still some uncertainty about their identity until someone recognised the banner and diagnosed the invasion as friendly. William was rowed ashore with much local rejoicing while at Cockington at the other end of Torbay a Catholic priest was just as happily celebrating the arrival of what he took to be the French fleet. By nightfall, however, when over 15,000 Dutch troops had landed the priest remembered the Vicar of Bray and did a quick change at a rate of knots.

The Dart

Seven miles down the coast from Berry Head you will find the Dart entrance, that is if you hunt about a bit, because though it looks wide enough on the chart it is surprisingly easy to miss in dirty weather or when you can't see the Day Beacon. There is nothing on this passage to worry about so long as you pay due respect to the East and West Cod islets, the Mudstone Ledge and the Druids Mare. Nearer the entrance you have the Nimble Rock and the East Blackstone to identify and a few unfriendly rocks on each side of the entrance, but the river will eventually open up when you are almost past it. By then Battery Point and Dartmouth Castle should be visible and you may, if you are lucky, have picked up one of the few buoys placed to keep you off the worst dangers. After that you are safe enough in the middle of the channels. As we know to our cost, the wind can be very fluky in the entrance and if there is much traffic – dare I suggest it – don't be too purist to hand your sails and motor if conditions are bad.

Though you may be too busy to appreciate it the first time in, this is a very beautiful estuary between steep cliffs which close in to a mere cable or two at the narrows. Once through the narrows you will have time to look about and you will see at once why this river was so important during all the centuries when we were at war, officially or unofficially, with the French, for this is the perfect harbour of refuge, with plenty of water at all states of the tide, excellent shelter once inside and yet easily defended by guns on both sides of the narrows. It was the assembly point in the twelfth century for the Crusaders' fleet which made its way across Biscay to the Mediterranean to meet Richard *Coeur de Lion* at Messina; and, to improve its defences it was granted thirty pounds a year by Edward IV to provide a 'stronge and mightye and defensyve new tower' from which a chain could be stretched across when unfriendly boats were around.

Now that you have got into the Dart I hope you will not be in too much of a hurry to leave, because there are nine or ten miles of this river to explore right up to Totnes itself and as we have said in the little bit of geological nonsense earlier, it is quite fascinating all the way. If your draught is too much to go right up to the top and you think it is a bit far for dinghy exploration you might do a lot worse than take a 'busman's holiday' up the river on one of the steamers which run three or four times a day if the tide serves and last year only cost 65p return. You will find the trip well worth while and for once it is rather restful to have no worries about going aground on the tricky bends especially near Totnes.

Now, I know most of us like to nose out pleasant anchorages for ourselves but unless you are open to a few suggestions you wouldn't have bought this book so, I will mention a few of our favourite spots.

First of all, you will of course want to have a look at Dartmouth itself and I would suggest that you go to one of the marinas here; there is one on each side and a ferry to take you across if you don't want to bother with the dinghy. Both Dartmouth and Kingswear are perched on the side of a steep hill. Seen from across the river the latter always looks rather continental and reminds me a little of Positano or Amalfi. Dartmouth itself still has some old houses with projecting upper stories while the *Royal Castle* Hotel is not only a gracious old coaching inn but will also give you a jolly good meal at a very reasonable price if the time has come to give 'cookie' a night off. They have a very reasonable wine list and are not fussy about dress. There is a little dinghy pool just outside for those who have come across the river in their own boat.

Next day you can sail up river through a beautiful wooded reach, though I am afraid only if the wind is favourable. The river is none too wide here and is so full of moorings that beating is really only possible for dinghies. You may fancy the anchorage opposite the Noss, but I would strongly advise you to go up to Dittisham, where there is good holding ground, the woods are very green and the *Ferry Inn* will feed you in a simple but agreeable way. On the way you will pass the Anchor Stone which is famous for two reasons. It is said to be the place where Sir Walter Raleigh smoked the first pipe ever lit in England and, perhaps more usefully, it was the place where the local men used to take their more difficult wives to cool off. Most of them were reasonably penitent by the time the rising tide reached their ankles, though a few of the tougher characters are said to have left it considerably later.

I should do your shopping in Dartmouth where there are good shops in a small radius, for you will not find many facilities at Dittisham – two little pubs and a post office which sells sweeties but, if you have the energy it is well worth getting up a thirst by walking up the hill, as far as you can, to enjoy a bird's eye view of the river with its twists and turns, its enchanting little creeks, impressive wooded crags contrasting with the green fields and the great sweep of brown hills away beyond Totnes to Buckfastleigh and the high tors of Dartmoor. If it is low water you will also, I suspect, be glad to get a look at the next reach, for from here onwards the river gets tricky and the great wide stretch just above Dittisham is a bit of a trap for unwary rookies. (The Stanford *Harbour Chart* H4 is a godsend here).

If you are lucky enough to find that you will have a rising tide that evening you might even call at the post office on the way down and phone the *Waterman's Arms* at Tuckenhay up Bow Creek to book a table for an evening meal. I can thoroughly recommend the experience. This delightful little creek runs up through woods, only has water for about two hours and is one of the most peaceful places I know. You tie up, if they will allow it, and they usually do, at the quay of the *Maltster's Arms* or that of Mannings Tuckenhay Cider Cellars next door. Here they still make draught cider and mead and it is only five minutes walk up the road to the *Waterman's Arms,* a low ceilinged old cottage apparently left behind in the middle of nowhere. They will give you an excellent meal there for only about 75p and you will just have time to get through it and back to your boat before the creek dries again. There are a few moorings up here off Stoke Gabriel, where there is another good food pub *The Castle* or a humbler one much favoured by yachtsmen called *The Victoria and Albert,* and a few more at Duncannon but there are not many places up this part of the river where you can lie afloat and you may have to creep back nearer Dittisham for the night if you want to be off at crack of dawn.

May I just warn you of one thing. On a rising tide don't go off and leave your boat anchored unless you are very certain that you really are off the fairway because, nowadays, Baltic timber ships of

400 to 500 tons go right up to Totnes. They may sometimes look a little out of place in the upper reaches of this river but at least their presence is causing some dredging and re-buoying so that more of the river is now navigable for yachts as well.

Totnes

It is always rather fun when old harbours come back to life, and Totnes, a walled town, was important at one time as a port as well as a market town. By tradition, however, and according to a rather suspect chronicler of the twelfth century, Geoffrey of Monmouth, it was also a town of great antiquity for Brutus of Troy sailed up the river about 2,000 years ago and landed here. Plymouth also claims the honour of this landing and embellishes the story with a wrestling match between the Trojan champion Corianaeus and a West Country giant, Gogmagog who was ultimately defeated and thrown into the sea. What interests me is that these improbable stories may well contain a germ of truth, even if a half educated chronicler gets most of his facts wrong. For a start, I think Geoffrey must have known that the West Country and Dartmoor in particular is littered with signs of a prehistoric population – the barrows, cromlechs and long avenues of stone leading to the menhir, a tall single stone. Some of them still exist and when Geoffrey wrote, before generations of local farmers had taken a fancy to them for building, they would have been even more plentiful. I am pretty sure that legends would have reflected the various waves of invaders, particularly the Celts who occupied this part of England after the Bronze Age. Like everybody else Geoffrey would have heard of the Romans and Brutus might have been the only name he could recall, other than those of the Emperors. I think the interesting point is that there must have been some firm tradition of a landing by an important traveller from the Mediterranean for the twelfth century historian to elaborate and the obvious candidate is of course the great sailor-scientist Pytheas who crept out of the Mediterranean about 320 B.C. and reached Land's End (Belerium) where he found,

> 'The natives of Britain by the headland of Belerium are unusually hospitable and thanks to their intercourse with foreign traders have grown gentle in their manners.'

From there he circumnavigated the British Isles landing at various spots to collect information about the population and their habits and fitting in a visit to Iceland on the way round.

Anyway you can drink his health in the *Seven Stars* or any of the pleasant inns in the picturesque old city of Totnes. The only annoying feature of the lounge bar in the *Seven Stars* is that they make you pay even for sandwiches in advance before they will cut them – perhaps they are allergic to yachtsmen or just dislike their fellow men, like an Irish barmaid who once surveyed me and the rest of a crowded bar in one comprehending glance and said, 'Cor, this dump wouldn't 'arf run a treat if it weren't for you lot always wanting things.'

Perhaps it is time we stopped speculating however and went back down the Dart. On the way you might like to notice two spots on the east bank. At Sandridge above Galmpton, John Davis was born and a little further down, Greenway opposite Dittisham was the home of Humphrey and Adrian Gilbert. We will come back to them and the story of the great English seamen of the sixteenth century when we get to Plymouth – you have had advance warning!

Even though it is rather crowded nowadays, I think most of us leave the home estuary of Chaucer's 'shipman' with certain regrets – illogical because there are just as enchanting places to come.

The Salcombe River

Rounding Start Point

Salcombe is about fifteen miles on round Start Point and here we do have to time our arrival because there is an unfriendly bar which is best crossed between half flood and high tide. There are no hazards on the way down coast but the Skerries can, like all shallow banks, produce an uncomfortable sea so it is as well to take evasive action. After Start Point it is a different matter; from here round to Bolt Tail you are on a dangerous coast and if fog comes down there is only one safe course – straight out to sea. I hope it won't be foggy for you because, apart from the worry, it would be a pity if you had to miss one of the most spectacular sections of our coastline. These great cliffs are of varying rocks, many of them volcanic in origin, with a range of colours and of those irregular, rugged shapes and steep faces that look really formidable. The cliffs are so steep that for long stretches there are few tracks down them. On top as you would expect, there are magnificent cliff walks and if you linger awhile in Salcombe there is a grand walk up Bolt Head and on part of the way to Bolt Tail if you have young and want to 'do them good' – how I used to hate being 'done good to!'

Start Point needs a wide berth, not only for outlying rocks like the Cherricks but also because of the race. You should be all right about a mile off and from here your next landmark, Prawle Point, will be coming into view. You can go in fairly close here and then make straight for Bolt Head with its curious spiky outline. There are some more Mewstones here and another group of rocks off Starhole Bay just north of Bolt Head, but so long as you are not too far west there are no dangers here until you pick up the leading line. Incidentally you can still see the remains of the barque *Herzogin*

Cecilie in Starhole Bay as a reminder of how not to come in. Between Wolf Rock and the Poundstone there is a turn to starboard for another leading line, but by this time the moorings will be in sight and the town of Salcombe itself, so the fairway will be obvious.

Salcombe

Like all these Devon estuaries, Salcombe is beautiful with its wooded, hilly banks, its little creeks (called Lakes here as in Portsmouth Harbour) for dinghy exploration and sandy coves which invite picnic parties, under the open downland above Portlemouth.

The town itself is attractive with its narrow streets and old houses and celebrated, locally at least, as the last place in Devon to hold out for the King in the Civil War. It is a warm spot with luxuriant, near tropical, vegetation in places which, I must admit, has made it a thought too popular in the season and the river almost resembles Piccadilly Circus with its rows of moorings narrowing the fairway and clouds of dinghies tearing about like demented butterflies. The trouble is that there is really not enough river to accommodate them all because from the main moorings above Salcombe (the Bag) to Kingsbridge is only three miles and even that dries out for much of the way, though vessels of nine feet can get up near high water. At one time, towards the end of the last century, Kingsbridge was a flourishing port with a Mediterranean trade which employed some 150 ships. Today its long quays lie empty except for the *Compton Castle,* an old paddle steamer finishing her life in a not very dignified way as a tearoom in a setting of little yellow muddy puddles that collect the afternoon sun.

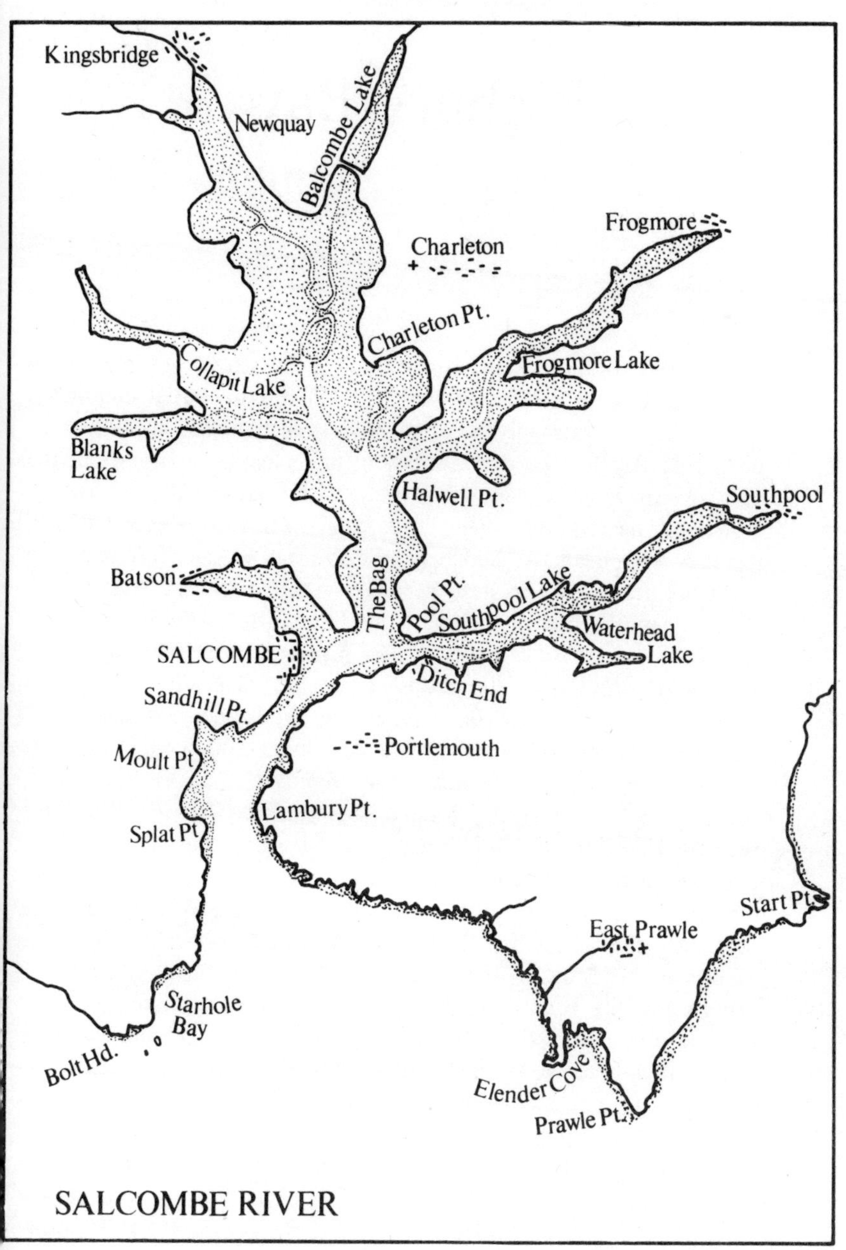

SALCOMBE RIVER

Bigbury Bay

If the wind is south westerly and at all strong you may from Salcombe have to go straight across to Plymouth, but if conditions are favourable I strongly recommend a little exploration in Bigbury Bay. This Bay had an evil reputation, understandable enough in the days of sail when a ship which got too far in would have had no chance of beating out again, though according to Frank Cowper, steamers have been wrecked here just as often as sailing vessels. The worst accident seems to have been the wreck of H.M.S. *Ramillies* in 1760, when she just sailed smack into the cliffs to the east of Bolt Tail. Only twenty-six of her 800 crew managed to scramble to safety. Ten years before that the troops had to be called out to prevent a 'Whisky Galore' episode on Thurlestone Sands, because this wreck attracted, not just a handful of islanders but 10,000 people from far and wide. In the next century the *Halloween*, one of the fastest sailing ships of her time, littered the shores of Sewer Mill Cove between Bolt Tail and Bold Head with a bank of wet tea leaves, the *Theodor* spread cotton seed along the shores and an early oil tanker the Russian *Blesk* started the new problem of oil pollution when she ran onto the Greystone Ledge in thick weather. The brigantine *Crossowen* hit Burgh Island in 1908 and the schooner *Sidney Smith* made a mistake at the mouth of the Avon four years later. Even so, there is still room for a few more – if you don't pick your weather!

But, not to worry, hell bent on simple pleasure as you are, you can afford to pick your weather, though even with a good auxiliary, I should give the popular wreck corner a healthy berth. This whole area between Start Bay and Bigbury Bay is known as the South Hams and the hinterland is still quite unspoilt; a charming area of narrow lanes, little secluded valleys with grey farmhouses tucked away cosily in some sheltered corner, and quiet villages with their low white cottages and thatched roofs. Going there by boat you could anchor in Hope Cove where the *Hope and Anchor Inn* will make you very welcome, though I wouldn't risk spending the night there, or even better, go up to Burgh Island and the Avon. At low water there are miles of beautiful sands here and you can anchor off Burgh Island while you have a noggin at the *Pilchard Inn* beloved by old Tom

The 'Pilchard Inn', Burgh Island.

Crocker, and then explore the river by dinghy. Or, if you are shallow draught and particularly if you can take the ground you could lead your way into what I think is the loveliest of all these rivers.

The Avon

I had better come clean and admit to an illogical nostalgic yen for this little river because of the many happy days I used to spend long ago with a retired naval friend, duck shooting and just pottering in a small sailing boat. When the weather was a bit too rough for a run to Salcombe or the Erme or even to the delightful little *Hope and Anchor Inn* at Hope Cove, we would come down on the tide from Aveton Gifford (pronounced 'Oughton') for an uproarious afternoon with old buddies at the *Sloop Inn* at Bantham. Afterwards, two very happy mariners would be escorted back to their little boat suitably supplied with emergency rations and the village would run a sweep on which muddy shoal we would finally run aground. All good clean fun – forty years ago. But, it does remind me to warn you that, lovely as it is, the Avon above Bantham is definitely a dinghy trip however shallow your draught. You will have spotted Bantham from the chart about a mile inside the bar.

You should have about twelve foot over the bar at H.W. Neaps and there is an eight foot pool opposite Bantham though with little room to swing, and a five foot pool up at Aveton Gifford. Tides can run up to six knots at springs and a careful study of the Pilot Guide is advisable, but once through the gorge like entrance the scenery is

The anchorage, Bantham.

really enchanting as you turn sharply to starboard, where you will see the two quays. They were once busy with the pilchard fisheries and their curing, and I have seen cargoes of lime, sand, coal and stone which were transferred into barges for transport up river. They even

Kingsbridge was once a busy port.

The entrance to the Avon River.

The Newton Ferrers Creek.

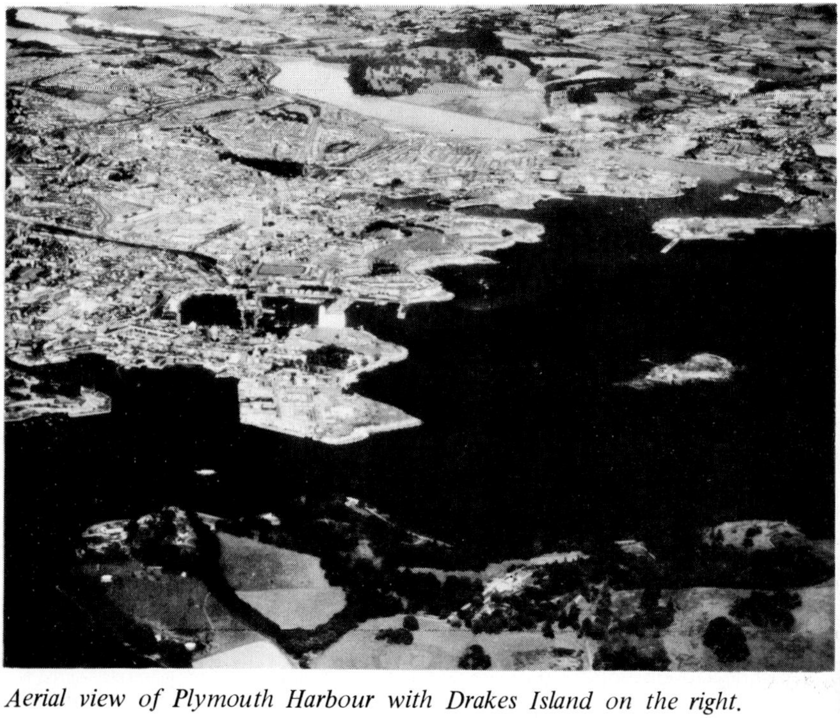

Aerial view of Plymouth Harbour with Drakes Island on the right. (Photo Aerofilms)

boasted a passenger steamer which arrived during the summer with visitors from Plymouth. An evening here would be well worth while, with of course a visit to the *Sloop* to meet some of the locals and listen to the soft Devon talk. Even the oldest inhabitant, however, can no longer tell you stories of the great days of the pilchard fisheries, when the Huer from the top of the Island spotted the shoals, the seine was rowed out while as many as forty horses and carts collected on the beach to carry the catch away.

I must not tantalise you further with talk about this river or the Erme to the North, which is just as lovely, just as difficult to enter and hasn't even got a pub, because it will be so rarely that you will find yourself on this coast when conditions are right, but if you are I do suggest that you find some way of getting to the *Journey's End* at Ringmore where Mr and Mrs Leger will give you a warm welcome and a meal that is out of this world at a price even we yachtsmen can still afford. In the middle of the summer you should telephone in advance to book a table, for the dining room is small and the inn popular even if it is in a remote little village on the way to nowhere. There are three other inns of great character and charm in the South Ham Area, though the food tends to vary a bit, *The Pickwick Inn, The Ebb Tide* and *The Dolphin.*

The Yealm

Most West Coast sailors drool reflectively at the mention of this river but, sadly I must say it, it is now getting distinctly mooring bound!

Approaching from the sea it is difficult to believe that there is any sort of navigable river running into Wembury Bay. The Bay itself, with its steep rocky cliffs has as background the wide semicircle which opens out between the projecting arms of Yealm Head and the local Mewstone – one of the largest of its kind and 194 feet high with its little brother of 48 feet lying alongside. The chart will warn you to keep well in the middle of this entrance, but with the church tower to give you a line, it is not too difficult to lead your way in to some comfortable corner for a temporary anchorage. It is only when you are well inside the Bay that the river entrance opens out, with a cottage and a pair of leading marks on Misery Point; these will get you past the bar which comes out from Season Point provided you never stray to the north of the leading line. To clear Misery Point you have to find a second pair of leading marks on the north bank. The Pilot books make it sound a lot more complicated than it is in practice, but I am not too keen on sailing in here as the channel is only one hundred yards wide and the wind is baffled by the high cliffs.

Before the yachting explosion, the Yealm was a delightful, peaceful river to visit, uninhabited except for the two little villages of Newton Ferrers and Noss Mayo up their respective creeks. Today I would regard it rather as a lovely place to live in for those who are young and fit. New bungalows have crept along the river bank above Newton Ferrers, but superbly placed up the steep hillside as they are, each can only be approached up a flight of fifty steps. Their garages are down across the road and below another flight of steps which leads also to a private landing stage for the dinghy. It is an attractive thought to have your mooring within sight of the house but I wonder if it would really mean more sailing – or would the garden win in the end! From these houses you look right up the river with its thickly wooded banks to Steer Point where it splits enticingly into two arms, inviting exploration at least by dinghy and in this reach you can see the river unencumbered by moorings because of the oyster beds. An added attraction is the water which is so clear that from the cockpit one can see the bass playing about among the stones.

It was of course inevitable that so lovely a place should have been discovered and smothered with desirable villas while below the oysterage the river meanders through the pattern of moorings. The harbour master, Mr Davis, tries to keep a little space for visitors, but it is one of the places where, if you are sure of your plans, it pays to phone in advance if you hope to go there at a summer weekend.

At low water you cannot get near either of the villages without a longish walk; they are joined then by a causeway across the creek. Of the two I greatly prefer Noss Mayo, which has remained a typical Devon village with its whitewashed houses clinging to the steep hillside while the old *Ship Inn,* a long rambling building squats down by the creek ready to revive sailormen when they come back home. Newton Ferrers too of course has its riverside pubs but it has suffered far more development than Noss Mayo and has lost much of its old world charm.

To see this river at its best you should go ashore and walk up to Yealm Head. Apart from that, there is really nothing to do except lead a quiet life aboard and possibly try a little fishing, or explore the upper creeks by dinghy. The navigable part of this river is short, narrowed by moorings and confined by high cliffs, so there is little room and often no wind for a day's sail, though the local sailing school manages to have some fun near the entrance. If a gale is blowing it is the perfect sheltered mooring; otherwise I should be inclined to look in for a lunchtime break only and go on round the corner to Plymouth for the night.

Plymouth Sound

Even after sailing for years I can't help feeling a suspicion of boyish excitement when sailing into any great harbour for the first time or even an old favourite after a long absence. In no other walk of life do the great and the small, the professional and the amateur rub shoulders so cosily. The yachtsman in his own little boat is as much master of his destinies as the captain of a liner or ocean freighter. I think this feeling is heightened in Plymouth Sound by the feeling that you are following in the wake of famous English seamen of the proud days of the first Elizabeth. Here the past merges naturally with the present and though our little cruises are so insignificant in comparison with the great voyages of the past, I have a sneaking notion that our feelings when we reach the home port after a bit of a dusting are not so very different from those of Drake and Hawkins when they limped in from the Spanish Main with a battered ship and an ailing crew.

Before we get too chatty about Elizabethan seamen and the Armada and all that, however, we had better perhaps give you a few facts about modern mooring problems. Plymouth Sound is a magnificent stretch of water some two miles square and with natural shelter from any direction except the south where a breakwater has been built half way up the Sound. At the head, it branches off into two arms, the Cattewater into which the River Plym flows in the east and the Hamoaze to the west, leading past the great naval dockyard of Devonport to the St German's River and the Tamar with its tributary the Tavy. For the first time since we got to Devon we have come to an area where there is plenty of room to sail in reasonably sheltered waters though of course the Sound is so large that even this will be interesting in near gale conditions and if you want to anchor you have to pick your spot according to the wind. The possibilities

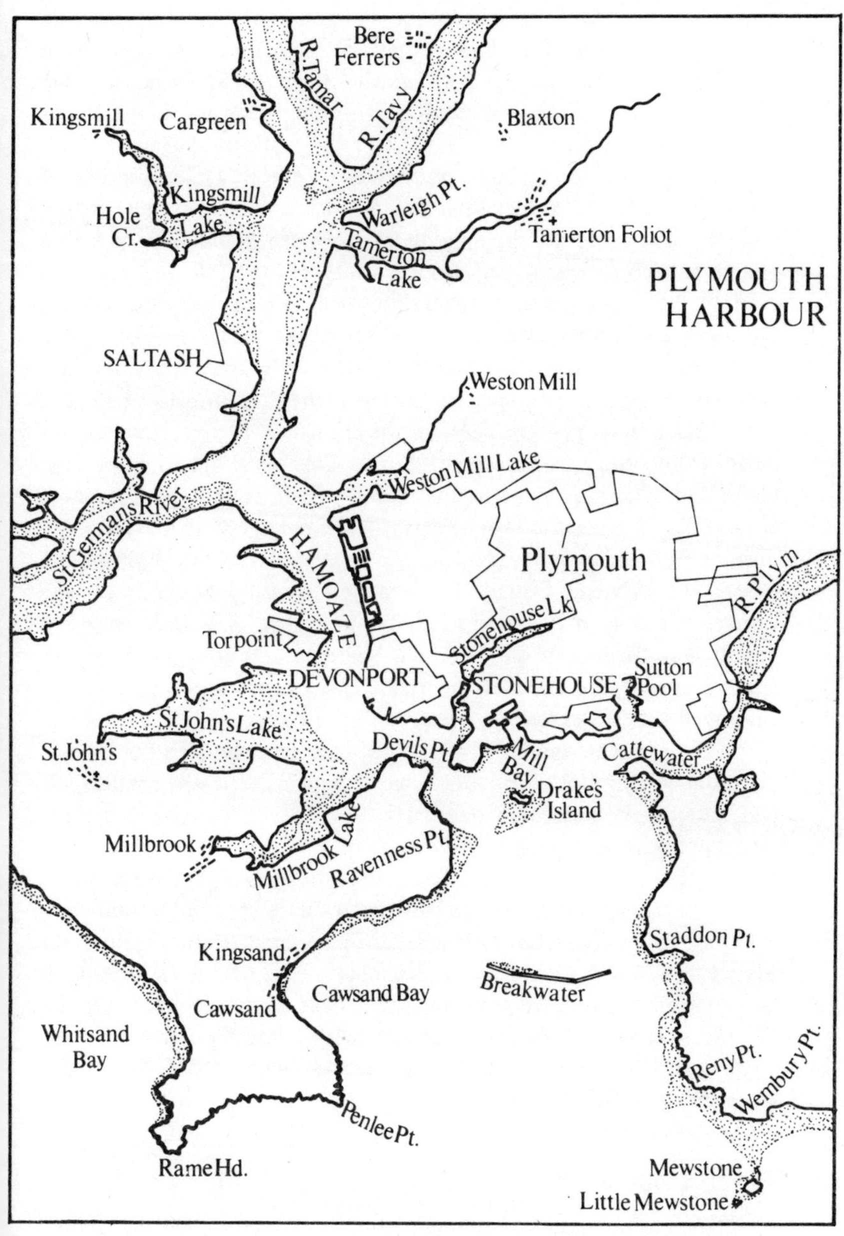
Bere Ferrers
R. Tamar
R. Tavy
Kingsmill
Cargreen
Blaxton
Kingsmill Lake
Hole Cr.
Warleigh Pt.
Tamerton Foliot
Tamerton Lake
PLYMOUTH HARBOUR
SALTASH
Weston Mill
Weston Mill Lake
St Germans River
HAMOAZE
Plymouth
R. Plym
Torpoint
Stonehouse Lk
DEVONPORT
STONEHOUSE
Sutton Pool
St John's Lake
St. John's
Devils Pt.
Mill Bay
Cattewater
Drake's Island
Millbrook
Millbrook Lake
Ravenness Pt.
Staddon Pt.
Kingsand
Breakwater
Cawsand Bay
Cawsand
Whitsand Bay
Reny Pt.
Wembury Pt.
Penlee Pt.
Rame Hd.
Mewstone
Little Mewstone

for mooring or anchoring are numerous – you will find them all listed in the Stanford Charts or Adlard Coles or the *Cruising Association Handbook* so I need only say here that they range from Mill Bay Dock or Sutton Pool in the town, where you can step ashore and find shops for your provisioning nearby, to the upper reaches of the Tamar.

Cargreen is one good spot where there is a pleasant inn to tempt you ashore. Above this, the channel is a bit difficult to find but you can go up on the tide as far as Calstock and with luck find one of the pools where you can lie afloat. On the tide you could go even further up to Weir Head Lock some sixteen miles on through the most spectacular scenery on the River, the great limestone gorge of Morwell. The only other possibility of getting away from the busy world of dockyards and bustling ferries, is the St German's or Lynher River. Like the upper reaches of the Tamar it is none too easy to navigate but you can anchor off Forder Lake with only a short walk up to the village, or right in the depths of the country in a pool off Earth Hill, or take the ground against the old quay at St German's, once a flourishing port and the site of the first Cornish Bishopric before the Norman Conquest. When St German was sent over the Cornish were enjoying themselves by indulging in a little innocent heresy and they gave the poor old Saint quite a rough time before chasing him to the cliffs at the Rame Head where angels arrived in a chariot in time to carry him away.

The mythical origins of Plymouth have already been mentioned. Fact starts with Domesday Book when Sutton, as it was then called, had about half a dozen inhabitants. By the end of the fourteenth century there were only three towns in England – London, Bristol and York – which had a larger population and Plymouth had a market, sent representatives to Parliament and was an important port, the base for official as well as unofficial expeditions against the French coasts and with room to assemble a fleet of over 300 ships. It was probably infrequent however for a fleet anywhere near this size to be assembled and ships in Plymouth mainly stuck to the Cattewater, the only part of the harbour with a narrow enough entrance to be defensible.

The Sixteenth Century Seamen

We are so used to thinking of ourselves as a maritime nation that it is a bit of a shock to remember how local our cruising was until about the middle of the sixteenth century. This does not mean that the Devon sailors, whether they were acting as fishermen or privateers, were not excellent seamen. If you want to indulge in a little gentle raiding of the enemy's coasts and harbours you soon learned to handle your boat very skilfully when the time came to make a quick get away. If your raids were on the Brittany coast you needed a bit extra. St Malo, Morlaix and Brest are specially mentioned as targets for the Plymouth corsairs and if you do not know the Chenal du Four, the short cut inside Ushant to get to Brest, or the rock strewn entrances to Morlaix and St Malo it only needs a quick look at a chart to appreciate the feat of seamanship involved. Even today when the dangers are marked by towers and lighthouses, beacons and buoys, the entrance to St Malo, with its dogleg channel and strong currents always gives me more than a little to think, if there is anything of a sea running. But, up to about the eighteenth century there were few navigational aids; the danger that these might help the enemy was considered far greater than the danger of shipwreck.

Today, in addition to the buoys and beacons, most of us would not dream of finding our way into harbours like St Malo without compass and chart. Both were in use in the Mediterranean by about the twelfth century, but the Northern countries generally did not hold with such luxuries and it is unlikely that our Devon seamen would have used either. If they were lucky, they might have a quick drawing of the important features on a crumpled piece of parchment, but it is much more likely that they had nothing but a few memorised instructions handed down from father to son. Apart from these they found their way by sun and stars, the feel of the wind, the look of the sea and, their one aid, a leadline.

While the Devon shipmaster's range was limited to coastal waters because he had none of the navigational skills needed for long passages across unknown seas, the Venetians had for 100 years been sending their 'Flanders galleys' to trade with our ports on their way to the Netherlands, and the Portuguese under Henry the Navigator were exploring regularly down the African coast. By 1520 Columbus had discovered America, Vasco da Gama had reached India and Magellan had circumnavigated the world. Apart from a desultory trade with Iceland by the Bristol merchants and their sponsorship of John Cabot's voyage to North America, the British had done nothing, and even Cabot was an Italian.

It was not until about 1550 that the British woke up and realised what they were missing. But they couldn't just sail off into the blue without preparation. The Spanish and Portuguese guarded their secrets closely in an attempt to keep a monopoly of their rich trade and, as usual, acquiring the necessary knowledge of ocean navigation was left to individual initiative. There is no room here to outline the somewhat devious methods by which the English managed to learn enough to make a start, but, as you will know, once they got going it was the Devon seamen who took the lead.

We have already met three of these *maestros* while coming down the Dart, Humphrey and Adrian Gilbert and John Davis. They, with the Gilbert's half brother, Walter Raleigh, from Hayes Barton near Budleigh Salterton, were enthusiastic about two possibilities – the colonisation of North America and the discovery of a new, quick route to China round the top of North America, the famous North West passage. Of these four friends the least known, John Davis is probably the greatest. It is not just that he made three great voyages to explore the unfriendly waters around the Davis Strait, setting out from Dartmouth in the *Sunneshine* and *Mooneshine* in 1585 and the next two years, for the immediate results of all these sixteenth century voyages were negligible in relation to the effort involved. What was much more important was that John Davis was a boffin as well as being a practical man and was the first Englishman to make a real contribution to international navigational theory and methods and indeed his textbook *The Seaman's Secrets* and his invention of the backstaff, (an instrument for taking sun sights) remained in use for more than 100 years.

While the Dartmouth men were exploring the unknown, their Plymouth counterparts were determined to penetrate the new lands of Spain and appear to have been more interested in trade and easy loot. This of course brought them into direct conflict with the Spanish fleet which was fast replacing the French as the national enemy. It has always seemed to me a little unfair on the Hawkins family, William, John and Richard, that in spite of their great contributions it was the adventurous but rather irresponsible Drake who became the popular hero – understandably enough for there was a puckish impudence about Drake which will always appeal to the English sence of humour. Who else would have thought of pushing off to sea without any charts, relying on his ability to seize what he needed from captured Spanish ships as he went along – taking the pilots as well for good measure? Even the Spanish, to whom he was the arch pirate had to admit to a reluctant admiration for his seamanship

To the inhabitants of Plymouth these Elizabethan sea captains were of course familiar and popular figures. They lived in the town and when at home could be met any day at the quays or walking on the Hoe. The whole life of the town was bound up with seafaring to such an extent that the beginning and end of each voyage was an occasion as important as the return of a single-handed navigator today. When Drake came back from the West Indies in 1573 he was tactless enough to arrive on a Sunday while everyone was in church. The messenger with news of his return emptied the Churches so that

> 'there remained few or no people with the preacher, all running out to observe the blessing of God on the dangerous adventures of the captain.'

For a typical send-off, the best account is perhaps that of Sir Richard Hawkins.

> 'When I left,' he wrote, 'the most part of the inhabitants were gathered together upon the Howe to shew their grateful correspondency to the love and zeal which I, my father and predecessors, have ever born to that place as to our natural and mother-town; and first with my noyse of trumpets, after with my waytes and then with my other musicke, and lastly with the artillery of my shippes, I made the best signification I could of a kind farewell. This they answered with the waytes of the town and the ordnance on the shore and with shouting of voices; which with the fayre evening and silence of the night were heard a great distance off.'

The Armada

We can hardly leave the Elizabethan seamen without some mention of their most spectacular success. There are many places along the South Coast where we might have talked about the Armada, many places where the population had a grandstand view as they stood on the cliffs watching the great Spanish galleons sail majestically through the Channel in their crescent formation, while the English boats herded them along like so many sheepdogs. On Portland Bill and from St. Catherine's Down they would have seen more actual fighting than from the Devon cliffs, while on the Seven Sisters the onlookers must have held their breath as the Spanish pilots spotted just in time the danger onto which they were being driven, the Owers.

But, it was at Plymouth that the English fleet awaited news of the Armada's arrival. It was a Plymouth man, John Hawkins who had been responsible for building and repairing the fleet and whose brother William, then Major of Plymouth who had seen that the western squadron was careened during the January and February spring tides and scraped and tallowed on both sides within twenty-four hours even though this entailed the expense of torches for the night work. It was from Plymouth too, that so many of the seamen must have come on this rare occasion when the more popular captains had no trouble in manning their ships – Drake it is said could have filled his two or three times, so great was his popularity.

The Plymouth Water Supply

There is one more connection between Drake and Plymouth which I should mention before we move on. In 1584 when he was the Member of Parliament for Bossiney in Cornwall the Plymouth Water Bill had been passed. It was a matter in which every sea captain would be interested when the alternative was to cart thousands of gallons in barrels from the surrounding countryside if a large fleet was to be made seaworthy. Despite the Bill, however, nothing was done for five years until Drake came to an agreement with the Plymouth worthies 'for the bringing of the River Meve to the town.' So, a seventeen mile long water course had to be cut and carried across the Burrator Gorge in great wooden chutes. In April 1591 when the work was finished Drake arranged for the Mayor and Corporation to walk out from the city along the dry bed of the Leat while he himself, in a scarlet cloak rode in to meet them at the head of the advancing water. This flamboyant gesture promptly produced the legend that he compelled a Dartmoor spring to follow his horse and come to Plymouth, but legend or not the water supply was real and well enough constructed to last for 300 years—a truly seamanlike effort!

The Third Eddystone Lighthouse

I think we can skip the *Mayflower* because every schoolboy has it all wrapped up, but before leaving we should just have a look at the lighthouse on the Hoe, which was transferred and rebuilt here. It was orginally the Eddystone lighthouse of John Smeaton which guarded the rocks from 1759 to 1882. You will remember that there had been two Eddystone lighthouses before this. The first was built by Henry Winstanley in 1696 and swept away in a storm together with the builder, his workmen and the keepers seven years later. The replacement was built by John Rudyerd of wood and stone and lasted fourty-seven years before it was burnt down. Smeaton, commissioned to build the third, decided on an entirely stone structure despite the fact that he,

> 'found it eternally rung in my ears from all quarters, that a Building of *Stone* upon the Edystone would certainly be overset.'

Any yachtsman will appreciate the problems of building a lighthouse on an isolated rock where the foundations are below high tide level so that there are limited hours when any work can be carried out in the early stages, and that only when the weather was suitable. Even in good weather you might go off to work and find that there is too much swell either to land or to work on the rock. In Smeaton's day such abortive expeditions must have been specially frustrating because getting there at all was quite an achievement. The Eddystone is a good fourteen miles out and in the eighteenth century there was of course no engine power – only sail and oars. Smeaton's own account of the building makes fascinating reading because, on the other hand, even fine days often meant they couldn't get near the rock for lack of wind. Let me quote his account of Tuesday, 19th April, 1756:

> 'The weather being very fine, clear and calm, we went out the fifth time for the Edystone; but the little breeze there was being right a-head, we tacked and rowed the whole day; and at night found ourselves about four miles from the rock. As the

> day was perfectly serene, we had the mortification of seeing everything calm and quiet about the rock, without being able to get near it. Upon the turn of the tide in our disfavour, we dropt anchor, in hopes of completing our voyage the next day's tide; but in the night it began to rain and blow so hard from the S.E. that we were glad to weigh anchor and come home; and in returning, the wind veering to the N.E. and blowing very hard almost right a-head, we had a laborious work in turning to windward and regaining Plymouth.'

This might be an account of any of our own cruises, but when you remember that all the workmen, their gear, materials and every block of stone had to be ferried out under such conditions it makes one wonder how the building was ever finished, let alone achieved in a mere four summers.

These conditions would of course make one fairly careful not to leave vital material ashore but we are all human and towards the end of the work Smeaton got out there to supervise the job of 'leading the door hooks into the jambs.' He found that

> 'They had unluckily forgot to send out a quantity of block tin, that I ordered, for the purpose of giving the lead a proper hardness, to prevent their shaking loose; to make, according to Mr. Rudyerd, a coarse kind of pewter. This was a disappointment, as it was one of the operations, the mode of which, I had in view to ascertain my coming out the last time; however, that I might not lose the opportunity, after some consideration the following expedient occurred to me; I melted down all the pewter plates and dishes that we could muster on board the buss, and mixing them with a proper quantity of lead, it answered my purpose.....'

The 'buss' he refers to here was moored off the rock and used as a store ship and sleeping quarters, small yawls being used to get them from there to the rock itself, where the landing place, the Gut, was rarely easy. In all the four years, however, there was only one occasion when the workmen were trapped on the rock and unable to get to the buss – a wet night but they 'amused themselves with their work; which, having their lanterns and candles, they were enabled to do.' Nights aboard the buss however cannot have been much fun and the first time the lighthouse was ready for habitation the men reported that they

> 'found it very warm and comfortable; much more
> so than the buss's hold and cabin.'

There were of course other hazards. The men were organised in two companies working alternative weeks and living on the buss so that they could work during every suitable tide on their tour of duty. Then as now, relief at the appropriate moment was not always possible and in October 1756 the loiterers on Plymouth Hoe were slightly surprised to see a 'little yawl...... with an oar for a mast, and a blanket for a sail' coming in gaily with three hungry seamen aboard.

Now and again they could not get back to Plymouth and had to run for Fowey and on one occasion, having missed that harbour in the dark and being nearly shipwrecked on the Gribbin Head, Smeaton and his crew found themselves drifting somewhere beyond Land's End with no chart or navigational aids. A friendly merchantman, who came by, gave them a course for the Scilly Isles, but at this moment the wind changed and blew them home. Difficulties of this kind one would expect, but soon the French couldn't resist taking a hand. They seem to have decided that they would not attack the men actually working on the rock – after all it was useful to them too to have a light out there – but this did not prevent their privateers making attacks on the boats bringing stone from Portland, added to which there was trouble from the Press Gangs even after the Admiralty decreed that this was a 'national service' and that the men employed on it would be exempt from the attentions of these gentlemen, because we hear of certain gangs trying to take off the best seamen even when they were aboard one of the lighthouse boats. However, despite all these problems, the lighthouse was finally finished, as Smeaton had promised, in four seasons. He must have been disappointed that on the night appointed for the official lighting-up the wind was so strong from the S.W. that no boats could set out from Plymouth to witness the great event. Three years later however the lighthouse had one of its biggest tests when it survived such a storm that,

> 'One of those who had been used to predict its
> downfal, was heard to say: if the Edystone

> Lighthouse is now standing, it will stand to the Day
> of Judgement.'

One hundred and eighteen years later a thorough examination showed that the tower was not 'defective or showing signs of decay'. It was in fact too strong, for it was the poor old Eddystone rock

Smeaton's Lighthouse now stands on Plymouth Hoe.

itself which was cracking up under the strain of carrying this structure. So, Smeaton's tower had to be replaced after all – but it may still last till the 'day of judgement' standing in honourable retirement on its new site on Plymouth Hoe.

Cornwall

We have of course been wandering in and out of Cornwall on our way up and down the Tamar, but to most of us these little riverside villages or the old ports such as Saltash and St German's are not quite the real Cornwall. I know there is a tendency to think of Cornwall as we knew it a long time ago with its rocks and high cliffs sheltering hidden coves and picturesque fishing villages, jammed in a cleft of the steep hillsides, with perhaps a few fishing boats hurrying home with the day's catch. And I know equally well that the picture has become a bit blurred by bungalows, bingo halls and 'sea view' tourist hotels. But you know, it hasn't really obliterated much. There are still the narrow alleys past houses with outside stairs and low doors leading to the mysteries of the cellar. The smells are still there and though the fishing boats are motorised, they still rush in to land their catches on cobbled quays while the painters paint and the tourists gape and the small boys and girls suck more expensive gob stoppers and choc ices, and it's just as much fun as it always was.

The determination of the Cornish to make their living from the sea is witnessed by the number of unlikely little harbours which have at one time or another existed. Between Cawsand Bay in Plymouth Sound and Land's End there are only two good natural harbours, only the two estuaries of Fowey and Falmouth are large enough to give safety and shelter under all conditions, and even those have certain little problems near the entrances. The Helford River should perhaps be included too, though it is exposed to the east, but the rest are artificial harbours, which mostly dry out and are horribly exposed to winds coming from one or more directions between south west and south east. As you will realise by now, a rocky coast is nearly always a dangerous coast and the south of Cornwall is no exception with its sharp headlands and outlying rocks. It was naturally more awkward in the days of sail when ships were apt to get themselves embayed, sailing hopelessly backwards and forwards for days, unable to make enough into the wind to weather either headland, and knowing that any attempt to anchor would be fatal. In Volume I of *Cornish Shipwrecks* the authors, Richard Larn and Clive Carter list over 700 wrecks in the area from Cape Cornwall to Plymouth between 1673 and 1966 and that of course is only recent history.

The Inner Harbour, Polperro.

The 'Smugglers House Hotel' at East Looe.

General view of Falmouth Harbour. (Photo Aerofilms)

Mousehole and the 'Lobster Pot' opposite the entrance.

Pilchard Fishing and its Harbours

Polperro

If it is dangerous out at sea, conditions inside some of these Cornish harbours may be little better with a gale from the wrong direction. Jonathan Couch has left this description of a storm in a local history of his native village:-

> 'In the time of a storm Polperro is a striking scene of bustle and excitement. The noise of the wind as it roars up the coomb, the hoarse rumbling of the angry sea, the shouts of the fishermen engaged in securing their boats, and the screams of the women and children carrying the tidings of the latest disaster, are a peculiarly melancholy assemblage of sounds, especially when heard at midnight. All who can render assistance are out of their beds, helping the sailors and fishermen; lifting the boats out of reach of the sea, or taking the furniture of the ground floors to a place of safety.... When the first streak of morning light comes, bringing no cessation of the storm, but only serving to show the devastation it has made, the effect is still more dismal. The wild fury of the waves is a sight of no mean grandeur as it dashes over the peak and falls on its jagged summit, from whence it streams down the sides in a thousand waterfalls and foams at its base. The infuriated sea sweeps over the piers and striking against the rocks and houses on the warren side rebounds towards the strand, and washes fragments of houses and boats into the streets,

> where the receding tide leaves them strewn in sad confusion.'

The worst storm in Polperro's history was in November 1824 when a half finished boat on the stocks was carried out to sea, three houses demolished, the inner pier, half the outer pier and fifty boats destroyed. But don't let me put you off, I hasten to add that the piers have since been improved and are now closed with baulks of timber in bad weather. This doesn't mean I am afraid that it is any sort of harbour to enter in southerly or south easterly winds or when there is much swell – you can just imagine the 'wash up' there is in an entrance only thirty-two feet wide!

Polperro.

Polperro, like so many is a typical fishing harbour with a history dating back at least to mediaeval times. It is true that fishing was often no more than a cover for the more lucrative business of smuggling, but as I said in *East Anglia from the Sea* I still don't think you want the statutory stories of routine smuggling. You can read them in any guide book so I will only just mention one outstanding character from further down the coast, John Carter known as the 'King of Prussia,' so impregnable had he made his own private cove with its caves, cliff path and fortress complete with gun which he had installed on the cliff – a very pretty set up which took Coastguards some time to dismantle.

In between smuggling and piracy or privateering, however, some fishing was done, particularly when the great shoals of pilchards came in between August and December. Then the fishermen from Looe, Polperro, Mevagissey, Polkerris, Gorran Haven, Portloe, Portscatho, Porthallow, Porthoustock, Coverack, Cadgwith, Mullion, Porthleven, Newlyn and Mousehole would row out the seine, a large ring net in which the shoals would be trapped in the shallow coves near each harbour. Later, drift nets became more popular and there was a certain enmity between the seine and drift men, but the seine has since disappeared. I can still remember in the 1930's the excitement when it was run out for mackerel and the excited crowds which gathered on the shore to see the size of the catch. But in the early days, the pilchard was the fish, as John Nordon, Surveyor of the Duchy of Cornwall from 1605-26 says,

> 'The moste commodious fishe and recheate fishinge is the leade fish, which is called a pilcharde; the commoditie that ariseth of this silly small fishe is wonderful.'

Looe

The industry was particularly flourishing at Looe and as you wander around the old, narrow streets with their whitewashed houses you will notice the doors leading down to the cellars. Here, when not needed for a more valuable cargo, the pilchards were preserved – in Tudor times by smoking, pickling or salting; later salting in bulk was the normal method of curing. This naturally was work for the women folk who, in the nineteenth century were paid 3d an hour and a glass of brandy. A by-product was the oil which was pressed out of the layers of fish and used in leather dressing, lamps, medicine and soap making.

You can see the sort of cellar where this work was done if you go to the Cornish Museum in Lower Street in East Looe. Much of the information above comes from an excellent little *History and Guide* written by its Curator, W.H. Paynter. You can also probably see a similar cellar if you go to the *Smugglers' Arms* in East Looe for dinner – and a really excellent meal you will get too at a very reasonable price. So we will hope that when you come past here there is no strong south easterly wind which makes the harbour impossible, and that the tide is high enough for you to get in. The harbour dries so you have to take the ground or lie against the quay, but if you don't mind that or being a bit of a peep show for the hordes of visitors, then I suggest that Looe is probably the most practicable of these fishing harbours for yachtsmen. Polperro is perhaps more picturesque and Mevagissey more unspoilt, but Looe has much more space against the long quays. It is a pity that there are not more of the old locally built luggers left – there are now only four out of a fleet of fifty.

I am afraid, again, I must admit to a great affection for Looe and would make for it every time. You wander in and find a bit of

A Looe Lugger in the harbour entrance.

quay, not, repeat not, by the fish market, or tie up to a fisherman having first made sure he is not leaving on the night tide. Then when you have snugged down and stepped ashore I will be surprised if you don't agree that there is something irresistably continental and gay about its narrow streets and water front. Even the women look half Spanish with their dark eyes and hair knotted in a neat bun. There is the logical inconsequence of Brittany, no cars are allowed to park in the open space at the back of the *Smuggler's Arms* as it is the only place the fire engine can turn, if it should want to.

If the restaurant is shut on one street you find a back door in the next which is always open and you enter an enchanting room which does duty as a lounge, a T.V. room, a bar, a reception desk and madam's private lair. After that you will be in good hands and a wonderful range of food and drink will materialise at the appropriate witching hour.

The harbour at night, when you eventually float back to your little yacht, is enchanting but take a back sight in daylight earlier, as all the narrow mediaeval little streets look the same after a good dinner and it is quite easy to get lost, temporarily. Next morning we see a couple of washing baskets in a van on the quayside – labelled 'Smuggler's Looe' – what fun!

Before you actually leave Looe and if you have the family aboard I am sure they will want to visit Looe Island, though it might be easier to do so in one of the local boats as tides run fast between Island and shore. Nearly a mile offshore and said to be the largest island off this coast, it really has everything – a natural rock swimming pool, secluded beaches, coves, caves, bird sanctuary, fishing, a collection of carved stones and gargoyles, smugglers' stories, a tearoom and a pottery. Its cottage was erected for the preventive men; earlier, there had been a cell for two monks but this is now vacant! The locals will tell you that Joseph of Arimathea went there with the boy Jesus, leaving the child on the island while he conducted his trade ashore – a very pleasant arrangement.

The Tin and China Clay Trades

I had better mention these, if only in self defence, before too many kind friends point out the omission.

Fishing and smuggling were not the only trades of these Cornish ports. Bad roads and the Tamar in the east virtually cut them off for centuries from the rest of England by land, and sea borne trade was therefore imperative. The Cornish tin trade as everybody knows dates back to the pre Christian era. I have already mentioned Pytheas, but long before he came to England the Phoenicians were conducting a regular trade in tin. How the Brythons of this corner of England discovered the art of extracting and working tin is as much of a mystery as the means by which the Phoenicians discovered their existence and the potential value of this metal, but it is clear that these early Cornish ancestors were no fools. They summed up the Phoenicians as pretty suspect characters and would not allow them ashore. Herodotus writing in 445 B.C. knew that this trade existed and Diodorus Siculus writing 300 years later has left us a good description:-

> 'They (the people of Belerium – Land's End) are singularly fond of strangers, and, from their intercourse with foreign merchants, civilised in their habits. These people obtain the tin by skilfully working the soil which produces it; this being rocky has earthy interstices, in which, working the ore and then fusing, they reduce it to a metal; and when they have formed it into cubical shapes, they convey it to a certain island lying of Britain, named Ictis: for at the low tides, the intervening space being laid dry, they carry thither in waggons the tin in great abundance. Hence the merchants purchase

> the tin from the natives and carry it across into Gaul, and finally journeying by land through Gaul for about thirty days, they convey their burdens on horses to the outlet of the river Rhone.'

Despite its extent, Caesar, when he arrived, was unable to discover the secret of this particular industry.

The island of Ictis is almost certainly St Michael's Mount. At some stage this trade must just have faded away as, in the Middle Ages, the ports of Mount's Bay, Newlyn and Mousehole, were nothing more than fishing harbours. The tin trade had by then moved to Hayle on the north coast, to Penryn, Devoran and Truro in the Falmouth area, and to Lostwithiel, Saltash, St German's and various minor ports on the Tamar. Lostwithiel and later Penzance were the only 'coinage' towns in the area.

St. Michael's Mount was the only port to retain its trade in tin and copper ore, the blocks being carted across the causeway right up to the eighteenth century. By then coal was coming into use and was carried back from the island to the mainland.

From the end of the eighteenth century, one further industry developed in Cornwall which was to depend essentially on sea transport because the product was a bulky and heavy material – china clay. If you have wandered about by car in the china clay area you can't fail to have seen what a mess they have made of the Cornish landscape with white slag heaps and pyramids of debris. As you probably know, china clay rock is actually a form of granite in which the felspar has been separated from the quartz etc., to form kaolin – that beastly stuff I remember having to take as a child. The best is found in the St Austell area so new ports sprang up or old ones were enlarged, the most important initially being Charlestown, Pentewan and Par. But you will scarcely need reminding that china clay ports are no place for yachtsmen. Indeed even a nineteenth century visitor to Charlestown writes,

> 'The smoke of its torment ascended in heavy clouds of black and white dust as we scrambled down the steep hill-side into the gruesome pit, where a crowd of undistinguishable beings are for ever emptying and loading an inexhaustible fleet of schooners. What the natural features of Charlestown originally were it is impossible to say, for everything is coated with white or black dust, and sometimes with both

together – on one side of the harbour vessels were being loaded with china clay, and their crews were as white as millers. On the other side coal was being discharged, and the crews were as black as Erebus. The villagers--- were black or white, according to which side the port they resided on. While some were both black and white, like magpies.'

Fowey

We're off to Fowey a bit further along the coast, though I can't resist mentioning on an enchanting paragraph in this morning's paper,

> 'The East Anglian Students Union voted Mr. James Reid the U.C.S. shop steward £200 for a lecture – this sum to be financed from profits of the Union contraceptive machine.'

I daren't comment!

It is quite a short run to Fowey and your Pilot books will give you adequate warning about the Udder Rock about half way along the coast. As you will remember, this is one of the two harbours of refuge along this coast which can be entered at any state of the tide, though even here I would not be too keen on using it with a big following sea as you would have to turn across the waves before getting a lee. Though it is unbuoyed, the entrance is not difficult provided you don't go too close to either side.

Once inside, you will be reminded inevitably of Dartmouth, with its two little towns, Fowey and Polruan facing each other across the river and climbing up the steep hillsides. The Dart may have more varied scenery, but they are both lovely rivers and like Falmouth and Looe, it is really a drowned river valley. The Fowey River however always seems to me rather a pleasantly sleepy place compared with the Dart and at first sight it is difficult to see why in the *Libel of English Policy* Edward III should have bracketed it with Dartmouth and Plymouth as one of the three ports he relied on to make war against Brittany. You will be even more surprised to learn that when it came to collecting ships for the seige of Calais, Fowey hit the jackpot for the whole of England. Dartmouth produced 32 and London 22; Yarmouth was well ahead of both with 43 but Fowey could beat even this high figure providing no less than 47 ships and

770 men; not all beer and skittles for Edward as the 'Fowey gallants' refused to salute the Cinque Ports and a grand old dust up ensued. It must have developed very rapidly as a port after the river to Lostwithiel began to silt up, leaving Fowey to inherit its valuable tin trade. From then on the town quays were busy with fish, salt, canvas, corn and timber from France, and outgoing pilchards and cloth as well as the tin.

There were the usual troubles with the French and the Fowey men became notorious for the ferocity and frequency of their own attacks on French shipping. These seem to have gone on quite happily for three or four years but then, by bad luck the new King, Edward IV, was inconsiderate enough to make peace with France and the French King was unreasonable enough to protest about the constant attack on his ships. Obviously Edward IV had to appear to play ball and sent his pursuivant down to Fowey to deliver a few well chosen words. Now, I suspect that if the men of Fowey had accepted a face saving reprimand they would have got away with it and probably carried on as before. But, they were a bit uncivil to the pursuivant and cut off his ears – which he resented and though Edward might have overlooked insults to his opposite number in France he felt this was a bit over the odds. The punishment was disastrous for the port. Not only were the ringleaders hanged or imprisoned and the town fined – that would have been normal and the town would have taken it as all in the day's work – but when they found they were also to lose their ships and to their traditional rivals the men of Dartmouth who were allowed to come round and collect them personally, they were speechless. Truro seems to have taken over the tin trade and Fowey folk had to get fishing again as soon as they had built a few new boats.

Even with the severity of this punishment it seems astonishing that it should have taken about 400 years before either official or commercial interests appreciated the rare value on this coast of a river that was always open for entry. It was not until the china clay trade started its boom and the search for suitable ports became urgent that the port of Fowey really re-emerged from obscurity. Now it is used by large steamers which come up to the new pier at Carne Point. To me these big boats look incongruous in this little Cornish river and the pretty reach up by Bodinnick Ferry is liable to be cluttered up with a dozen or more of these monsters moored right up the river. The impression that these freighters have somehow got left over from a commercial film is enhanced by the fact that from Fowey itself and Polruan Pool there is often no sign of this commercial activity and apart from the change from fishing boats to modern yachts the river looks as it has done for centuries. The narrow cobbled streets, too narrow for footpaths, are still there and so is the *Ship Inn,* redolent of privateering days. But, for me, Fowey will always have a nostalgic attraction as the home of my very loved

Place House and the Church, Fowey.

old tutor Sir Arthur Quiller Couch who lived here, when not at Cambridge, in 'The Haven'. On Sunday evenings at Cambridge about sixteen of us would cross the road from St Johns, to the Divinity school where this gentle old spinner of legend and good talk would hold us spellbound for hours over coffee. However far the talk ranged over literary and current topics of the day we would eventually lead him back to his native Cornwall where he was ever at home bringing its myth and legend to life in his own quiet, humourous and gentle way. I like to think that he must have had some notion of the abiding pleasure he gave to those few casually collected undergraduates of long ago.

From Fowey to Falmouth

Mevagissey

If the wind is suitable we can look in at Mevagissey, which we have already mentioned, on the way to Falmouth, but as it is only a few miles down the coast it is little help in shortening the passage to Falmouth. It is still a fishing village and in the outer harbour you may find room to lie at anchor so long as you keep clear of the nasty looking rocks round the edge, and there is no onshore wind. Then the outer harbour is quite beastly and there is no refuge up river which almost dries out. Perhaps that is why the locals come down with the parson on St Peter's Day and bless the waters and pray for fish!

Offshore Dangers

So you are in for a long trip of thirty miles or more to Falmouth because in the stretch of coast from Dodman Point to St Anthony Head there is only one spot where there is even a pretence of a harbour – at Portscatho in Gerrans Bay and that, as Adlard Coles says, provides no more than a temporary anchorage outside during offshore winds. You can't even enjoy yourselves on this trip, pottering along the coast because at Dodman Point you will be well advised to keep two miles offshore to clear the overfalls, at Nare Head there are the Whelps to avoid and further down The Bizzies with more overfalls both there and off St Anthony Head. So for most of the day the land will be no more than a distant blur and if the wind is adverse which is very likely on a south westerly course you may have your work cut out to beat down to Falmouth in daylight.

The Falmouth Estuary

Once you have got safely into the harbour however – and the entrance is not difficult – you will have no doubts that Falmouth is one of the best sailing areas in the country. It is not just that in the Carrick Roads you can enjoy a magnificant stretch of open and reasonably sheltered water, the joy is that the area offers so much variety in its ships as well as its scenery. Large modern coasters still anchor in the Carrick Roads – and beside them in winter the fleet of local oyster boats – some thirty of them and still working under sail.

St. Mawes

You can sail to St Mawes which, protected by its steep rocky banks nestles in a bight of the Porthcuel River and looks out onto a pastoral scene. You will get a good meal here at the *Rising Sun,* or better still you can join the locals at the *Victory* for a lunchtime drink and good snacks. The anchorage off the town is very exposed to the sou'westers but the upper river has enough bends to provide shelter under any conditions. There is only one snag; St Mawes I'm afraid is the most popular spot in the whole of this area so unless you are lucky enough to find a free mooring you may have a very long dinghy ride if you want to come ashore.

Falmouth and Flushing

Falmouth itself is an attractive town with its eighteenth century terraces, once the home of the sea captains and beyond the docks you will probably find that the helpful Royal Cornwall Yacht Club boatman will produce a mooring. I would always want to look in at Falmouth, if only for a lunchtime halt and hope to catch the water barge and fill up my tank and it is of course the right side of the river in a southerly wind. But if possible I really prefer the little town of Flushing on the opposite side of the creek where the *Seven Stars* will feed you in the sailing season.

Penryn

From Flushing one can run up with the tide to Penryn, the old port for the area, much older than Falmouth, where ships used to come for provisioning and cattle were brought up in barges to be slaughtered on the spot and taken to the local tannery. There is talk of building a marina up here. If it comes about it would be a good place to lie and you could be assured of a warm welcome from Kathleen Fawsitt, the new hostess of the *Anchor Hotel* and if she tempts you to expose yourself to one of her 'out of this world' steaks, I advise you to fall for it.

It is an old place the *Anchor,* at the head of the creek where small coasters still go on the tide to dry out against the Town Quay, or Exchequer Quay as it is now called – the sole point of Customs in former days when the trade was in tin, copper, oysters and granite. The inn is wedged in between an engineering shed and the tannery and a gentle odour of tanning still pervades the bar when the wind is in the right direction. But it doesn't interfere with the delight of listening to the Pakistani chef waxing lyrical over the delights of 'Hoome med Coornish parsties'.

When we were last there the whole establishment was alight with a wedding party for a sailor boy who had long since ceased taking much interest in his surroundings and a blond poppet who was only interested in seeing that the Juke box was up at full strength. Small boys were solemnly stuffing the bunches of friesias into their pockets and chocolate buns into their mouths. The *hors d'oeuvres* had been regarded with grave suspicion and given a wide berth. But, as our hostess said resignedly, 'They seemed to be enjoying themselves.' Outside you could hear the curlews and oyster catchers in full chorus. One thing I must warn you, if you have a yachtsman's yen for a good bath you will encounter the former proprietor's sense of humour. There is a bath, but it was apparently built for a retired leprechaun who had been dropped at birth. It is not merely that you have to wrap your legs round your neck to get in lengthways, but sideways you stick half way down the bath. In that posture I found it quite impossible to do any washing except the tips of my ears but was lucky to wriggle myself free and achieve a stand-up splashabout. It was afterwards explained that visitors by motor car 'don't seem to want to splash about much!'

Mylor and Restronguet

But we must get on with the job and give you a few really delightful spots to explore on this estuary before a final word about Falmouth itself. The open waters of the Carrick Roads extend for a further three miles to the north and off them run a series of little creeks, Mylor and Restronguet on the west and St Just on the east. Like all well known anchorages, they have been promptly and systematically filled with moorings by the locals, so you may have to hunt about. Mylor, however, is a good base with its quay, dockyard, good shops and cafe/restaurant which is considerate enough to stay open late for tired yachtsmen whose wives have told them what they can do with the galley. A little above the Restronguet Creek the banks close in to give you another change of scene and you have a lovely river to explore.

Restronguet on the old Post road to Truro may amuse you. The old row boat ferry has been in operation for five hundred years and there is one of the few old thatched inns in Cornwall. Originally the *Passage House Inn* and later bought by the captain of the ship sent to search for the Bounty mutineers, it is now well known as the *Pandora Inn* and is worth a visit though it isn't everybody's cup of tea.

There is a good anchorage in the wooded reach just above King Harry's ferry, about quarter mile up where a slipway on the west bank gives a good landing at any stage of the tide.

Malpas

Just above this there is a fork where the Fal itself goes off to the east and degenerates into a shallow creek only navigable for a

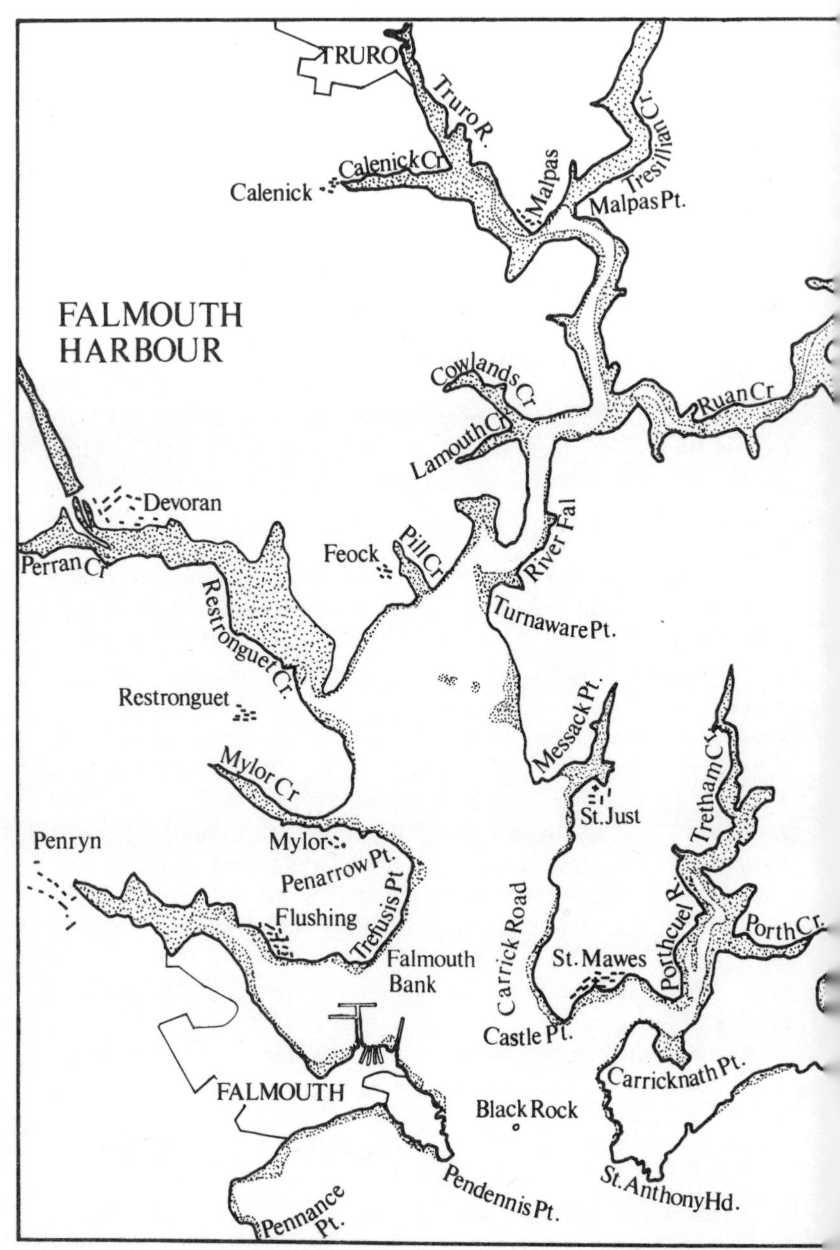
FALMOUTH
HARBOUR
TRURO
Truro R.
Calenick Cr.
Calenick
Malpas
Tresillian Cr.
Malpas Pt.
Cowlands Cr
Lamouth Cr
Ruan Cr
Devoran
Perran Cr
Feock
Pill Cr
River Fal
Restronguet Cr.
Turnaware Pt.
Restronguet
Messack Pt.
Mylor Cr
Tretham Cr
St. Just
Penryn
Mylor
Penarrow Pt.
Trefusis Pt
Flushing
Porthcuel R.
Porth Cr.
Falmouth
Bank
Carrick Road
St. Mawes
Castle Pt.
Carricknath Pt.
FALMOUTH
Black Rock
Pendennis Pt.
St. Anthony Hd.
Pennance
Pt.

short distance, but the Truro River still has plenty of water right up to the Malpas (Mopus to the locals, and to you if you want to be understood!) Point where, even nowadays you may be able to anchor for a few days and see no other boats. You can get a bus from here up to Truro, or better still take the boat up on the tide for, as you approach up river, the cathedral spire dominates the scene in much the same way as the much more famous spire at Amiens when coming down the Somme. Malpas, I would have said, many years ago was one of the prettiest and most romantic spots in Cornwall (it is riddled with Tristan and Iseult legends being where she crossed to her waiting boy friend on the other side) but though the birds and woods are still there I'm afraid it has got a bit curate's eggy with time. Old Jenny Mopus was a more recent and robust character to my mind. She died at 82 in 1832 and was for most of her life the mistress of the 'Happy-go-Lucky' passage boat. She always declared her worst passengers were 'Wemmin and pigs.'

Falmouth in its Heyday

Anyway, you could almost spend a whole summer quite happily in these waters and never get bored. The surprise is, once you have discovered this magnificent natural harbour, that Falmouth itself is comparatively modern. The old ports were Truro and Penryn and when Sir Walter Raleigh put in here on his way back from Guiana he found nothing but Arwenack, the big house and one or two cottages. Impressed by its possibilities he persuaded the authorities to back his scheme for development and the local landowner, Sir John Killigrew was quick to take advantage of the possibilities. It may be that he was in need of something to restore his reputation for he and his servants who took the blame had been involved in some pretty suspect business involving kidnapping and piracy about this time. Despite the natural opposition from Penryn and Truro the new port developed steadily. By 1688 its original name of Smithick and its temporary nickname Pennycomequick had been changed by royal proclamation to Falmouth, a market had been instituted, the Custom House moved from Penryn and a quay built.

It was the discovery of the New World that made Falmouth and it became the natural base to choose when in that year the Post Office established its Packet service, a fleet of fast boats sailing regularly from Falmouth to foreign ports and the colonies. Lisbon, Gibraltar, New York, Charlestown, Barbadoes, Jamaica, Brazil and Surinam were among the destinations of the packets, sailing weekly to European ports and monthly to the more distant parts. Carrying nothing but passengers and mail, they had the right to fly pennants as ships of war and their commanders were ranked as naval officers. They were built for speed and could outsail most enemies, though there were certainly occasions when they were glad of their guns and a few famous fights in which they were involved.

This was rumbustious Falmouth's heyday when the quays and ale houses were packed with brawling seamen and hopeful emigrants and bargains were struck over lean Spanish cattle, Stockholm tar, St Petersburg tallow, Stettin hogsheads, dogfish oil not to mention red herrings, hessians, dowlas, drills, ticklinburghs, Carolina cotton, Cork butter, French brandies, ruffs and laces, furs, velvets, precious stones, tamarinds and sweetmeats and even fripperies like fans, ostrich feathers and silver fiddle strings – Whow!

As to events of world importance, why, of course Falmouth heard of them long before London itself from the troop ships, packets, battle boats and convict ships for which it was the first inward port of call.

For the best part of two centuries the packets sailed from Falmouth and it was not until steam replaced sail that the service was transferred to Liverpool and Southampton. The packets were not the only ships to be found in Falmouth Harbour. With the uncertain length of voyages under sail, it was clearly a wise precaution to refill with food and water at the latest possible moment on the outward journey and it might be a pressing necessity to do so as soon as possible when coming home. With Falmouth the obvious point of call, the practice arose of calling there for orders, and on the homeward journey this was especially important as the port where cargoes were to be discharged was usually not fixed until the time of arrival could be estimated with some certainty. This practice remained until about the middle of the nineteenth century when a signalling station was set up at the Lizard to give the ships the information they needed. Anyway, if you are wandering round, I advise a visit to the *Chain Locker* on the quay. This is the pub used by the locals, and after all, they should know.

The Helford River

From Falmouth, however idle you may feel, there is another short cruise which you really shouldn't miss, to the Helford River. Don't go there if the wind is easterly because you will find no sheltered anchorage, but under any other conditions I can thoroughly recommend this beautiful, peaceful river which you can enter at any state of the tide and without any difficulty if you take ordinary care about the two offlying clusters of rocks, the Gedges and the Voose. Once in the river you can anchor near the entrance off Durgan, or go on to Helford when the village is only a short walk, or why not look in at the *Ferry Boat Inn* for a meal on the opposite bank at Helford Passage. There are delightful creeks to explore, though the best of them, Porth Navas, with its little pool called Abraham's Bosom, and Frenchman's Creek are nowadays rather plastered with moorings. At high water you can go up another creek to Constantine or further up the river itself to Gweek, in medieval times the port for Helston. These expeditions are of course best done by dinghy. Everywhere you will find wooded banks and little villages with white washed cottages nestling in sheltered hollows. To see this river and its creeks at their best, you really should climb the steep hillsides and look down on them. One of the best vantage points is above Porth Navas on the road to Constantine and it is well worth the walk even though it is a bit of a sweat. I don't suppose you will, but there is no harm in suggesting it!

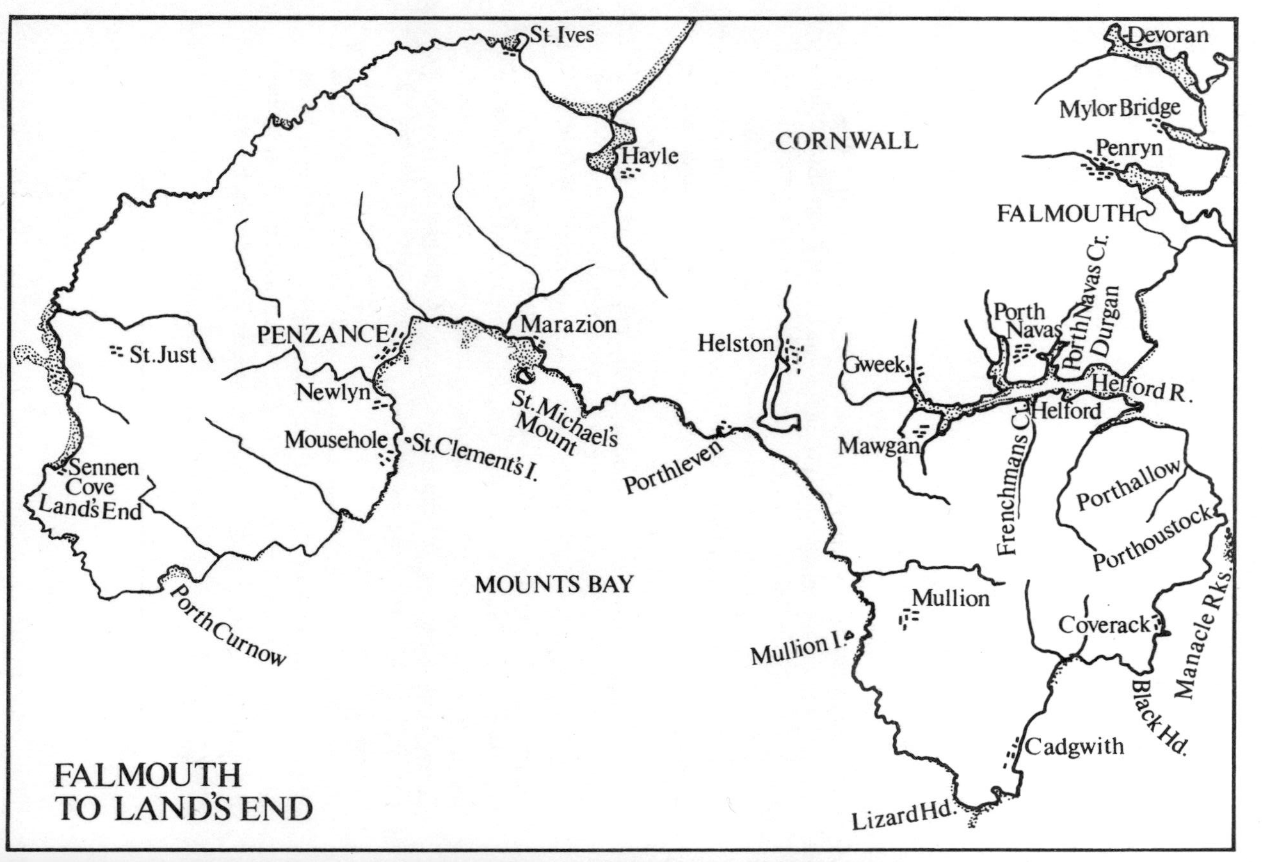

FALMOUTH
TO LAND'S END

The Lizard and Mount's Bay

For many yachtsmen the Helford River will be the end of their Cornish cruise, for you need I think to be a bit of a keen type to venture round the Lizard into Mount's Bay with its collection of somewhat doubtful harbours. It is a good day's sail to get there, of about thirty miles or so with a dangerous group of rocks, the Manacles, soon after you leave the Helford River and more rocks and a race to contend with off the Lizard. In passing, you can reflect that the Manacles has the best collection of wrecks on the whole Cornish coast and that is quite something in this part of the world. If you are a glutton for punishment and pretty ports you can call at Coverack cove with its tiny, drying harbour or, on the western side of the Lizard peninsular, at Mullion with an equally small and picturesque harbour, but neither of these is really suitable even for a night, as they are both too unpleasant inside if the wind plays 'silly boys'. A better possibility is Porthleven, north of Mullion, where there is a fair amount of room to dry out against the quays in the inner harbour – that is if you have got in in one piece, for this entrance is one of the nastiest I have ever seen, with rocks extending from the end of the pier, great sloping beds of them on both sides of the outer harbour and no buoys or leading marks to help you find your way in. So, without wanting to sound even faintly discouraging I really suggest one of the four main harbours at the head of the Bay, St Michael's Mount, Penzance, Newlyn, or Mousehole. Of these, Penzance is commercial and only possible for yachts if you lock in to the inner basin, Newlyn is a busy fishing port, Mousehole tiny and dries out as does the rather larger St Michael's Mount. We will look at them a bit more closely in a minute, but for the moment, as we cross the bay, a word about this corner of England, for we are approaching the most legendary part of Cornwall. It is an area where even the truth can be a bit surprising. We are used for example to hearing of coastal towns sacked by the French, and it may not even surprise us to learn that seven years after the Armada business the Spaniards got loose again in these parts and destroyed Newlyn, Mousehole and Penzance. But it really does seem a bit unreal to hear in the seventeenth century of the danger from Turkish pirates, not once but several times in Mount's Bay, round the Lizard and off the Manacles. They were actually Barbary pirates and Sallee rovers, but no less dangerous for that. In one year they collected 100 Cornish seamen; on a single day in 1636 they got 7 boats and 240 fishermen and two or three years later Sir John Pennington saw,

> 'Five sail of Turks men of war standing in for the Channel... clean, light, nimble vessels, and would have done a great deal of spoil, and made many a poor soul captive.'

I am sure that most of England thought Charles I was exaggerating when he tried to raise Ship Money

> 'Because it is given to us to understande that Certayne Theeves pyrates and Robbers at sea, Ass well Enemyes to the name of Christ, as other Mahomitans haveinge gathered togeather shipps and the goods and Merchandize not only of our subjects, but alsoe of the subjects of our freindes at sea ..... wickedlie takinge away and spoylinge them at theire pleasure, have carryed away, And the men in the same into miserable captivitie takinge...'

The Cornish seamen at least, were labouring under no illusion.

There was another odd period on this coast when troops had to be brought in at Penzance and Newlyn because of a ding dong between Cornish and East Anglian fishermen. It was not that the Cornish minded the Lowestoft and Yarmouth men coming south – they themselves went up to the North Sea during the herring season and similarly laid about them. But the Cornish at this period were 'Sabbath-loving people' and stuck firmly to their principles, even when it meant missing Monday's fishing as well, because of tides or letting a shoal of the precious pilchards go by. So their anger was understandable when the ungodly East Anglians deliberately brought their fish in on Sunday or early Monday morning to capture the market for the week, and any means to prevent them from landing their catches and forcing them to throw them back into the sea were regarded as legitimate. At this stage St Ives was the leading fishing port in Cornwall though it was supported by Newlyn in this battle. As late as 1929 there was a riot at St Ives on the question of Sunday observance and even today the port is closed on Sundays. They paid a high price for their principles and the canny Newlyn men have long ago given the parson second best and, as a result, replaced St Ives as the premier fishing port in Cornwall.

We should not, however, really be surprised at anything that happens down here when we remember that the area is still not quite normal; as you know it was the home of giants, witches, and mermaids and even the best of them are apt to get a little temperamental at time. I mean, take the heavy concentration of wrecks shown in Mount's Bay and round the Manacles. The purist might quite easily fall into the trap of supposing this was caused by fog and gale and unfamiliarity with the dangers of the race off the Lizard, when standing in to read messages – the signal flags at the Lizard signal station. Perhaps only the Cornish are really aware that the end was, in most cases, a foregone conclusion because the storm had been brewed by the Witches of the Logan Stone especially their Queen Bee, Madgy Figgy, who used to sit on her great basalt chair on the cliff at Tol-Pedden-Penwith and watch the struggling boats until she could fly off on her stem of ragwort to join the neighbours in plundering the wreck. The old hag lived in a cottage near Raftra and her gang, which was fairly numerous, accounted for a great number of wrecks including a Portuguese East Indiaman which she lured into Perloe Cove. She drowned the passengers and her buddies stripped the corpses as they were washed ashore. The harvest must have been a good one for the country lassies wore rich dresses for years to come and the village dripped jewels as these and gold continued to turn up on the beach following onshore winds.

We are sailing now over the Lost Land of Lioneese where they say there were once 140 parish churches and great forests with a few mountain peaks where we now find the Scillies. In some parts of Mount's Bay, beech trees are reputed to have been found with nuts clinging to their branches. The Saxon chronicle indeed records great floods which 'drowned many towns and mankind too innumerable to be computed' in 1014 and again in 1099, while local legend tells of one, Trevilian, who rode before the flood on a great white horse and escaped. The geologists would agree that the Scillies were once part of the mainland and that the land between has since been drowned, but they might be inclined to date this a few million years before the Saxon chronicle. They would also explain St Michael's Mount in the same way, though only the Cornish know how wrong the experts can be, for St Michael's Mount was actually built we are told by the giant Cormoran who selected the great granite blocks carefully from the neighbouring hills and then roped in his poor wretched wife, Cormelian, to carry the heaviest loads. The place must have been stiff with giants in the giant season and the locals must have been pretty busy keeping out of their way. Indeed, it was a friend of Cormoran

St. Michael's Mount.

who built the great castle on Trecobben Hill over towards St. Ives. These giants were often apparently a bit hard up as they only had one cobbling hammer between them. However they could share it easily enough, by just throwing it from one to the other across miles of countryside like Thor, that is until Cormoran's short sighted wife rather spoilt things one day by putting her head in the way with unfortunate results.

Nobody around these parts would try to keep a boat in Porthcurno Cove, near the Logan stone for it was here that the black, square rigged ship sailed straight ashore, bringing a strange man and his servant who used to go out fishing in all weathers until, on the old man's death, servant and boat both just disappeared. Everybody around knows the power of tears, that the Tamar is really the lovely nymph Tamara who dissolved in tears and the Tavy and the Taw the two giants who were her lovers though one, in searching for her, went in the wrong direction. Everybody knows too that you must never harm a mermaid; at Seaton near Looe and at Padstow they took their revenge by filling the harbours with sand. On the other hand after a little intensive petting they were inclined to become pretty accommodating.

We don't seem to have done the 'little people', as the locals call them, very proud but that doesn't mean they aren't still very active feasting and doing good works after dark. If you don't personally come across them during your cruise – and I am bound to admit to you that very few of my friends seem to be on the right wave length – you can be sure they are away round the corner busy about their proper business of combing the goats' beards ready for Sunday, or putting flowers on Merlin's tomb or turning water into wine or, why not, just dancing round the market cross on warm summer nights – so mind where you put your feet as you come out of the little pub on the quay tonight if you want to avoid a quite unaccountable piece of bad luck.

I think the little people still enjoy themselves, but these days they have become thinner on the ground than the local saints – partly because, I am reliably informed, many of them have now been converted to Christianity.

One thing you must see is their gardens and the best ones are in the Land's End area. If you go down as far as you can on the south west side of the Logan Rock Cairn and look carefully over the edge, you will see lovely little sheltered places of green: these are their private gardens, beautiful with cliff pinks and slender ferns where they can enjoy the sun and cultivate the wild sea asters and golden samphire.

Penzance Bay – Newlyn and Mousehole

I'm afraid this is our last bay on this trip. If the tide is low we shall have to go in to Newlyn, that Walberswick of the West, and if you can take the ground you will not be too uncomfortable there, though there is bound to be a good deal of disturbance as the fishermen come and go. If you want to stay afloat, the harbour master will do his best for you, but this is a busy fishing harbour and the casual yachtsman is not really welcome for a long stay. If the tide is high you could creep into Mousehole, that tiny, nearly circular harbour, a few miles on, which dries out and is surrounded by grey granite cottages. You tie up to the breakwater here and could spend a pleasant day or so, looking in at *The Ship* at lunchtime to meet the locals and trying the nearby *Lobster Pot* for a really sumptuous, if pricey, evening meal. In suitable weather you can anchor outside between St Clement's Island and the breakwater and as the tide goes down, watch flocks of little black and white birds flying in through the harbour entrance low over the water. You may not recognise them in flight, but you will as soon as you see them busily at work at the water's edge. They are turnstones which come here to join the oyster catchers and gulls.

Penzance

Penzance is mostly commercial but more and more yachtsmen seem to use it. I think it is quite a possible 'pop in' for a night but not, of course, in a southerly wind because of the shoal water outside and even if you get in in one piece the lock gates of the river basin cannot always be opened. If there is a gale, find somewhere on the north pier, coal dust and all, as the waves tend to bounce over the southern pier and you can get very, very wet.

St. Michael's Mount Harbour

Personally, if I wanted to stay around the Bay for a few days, I would always go for St Michael's Mount rather than any of the other possibilities. Most of us find islands fascinating and one which is joined to the mainland at low tide is even more so. The harbour is quite comfortable with reasonable space to dry out against one of the quays but if you want to remain afloat in about nine feet you can do so about a cable west of the northern end of the west pier. There is nothing much to do on the Mount, no amusements and no facilities except water, and even Marazion, which you can walk to at low water is a dour little town. But if you just like to swim, or to enjoy the life of the seashore, then St Michael's Mount is the place for you and it will be a whizz with the kiddywinks! There are rock pools to explore, oyster catchers, turnstone, godwits and green sandpipers to spot among the rocks and along the salt marshes and at the cliff edge you may find the greyish bulrush, the sea kale, the yellow horned poppy, the sea holly which is particularly fine here and the tall sea

Fishermen sorting their catch in Newlyn.

radish flourishes along with the commoner plants like the sea spurrey and the sea aster. Up the cliffs you will probably come across thrift and the rock samphire with the white sea campion and if you are lucky a great bush of tree mallow with its deep pink flowers. Wild thyme, stonecrops and red campion mingle with the yarrow, scabious, thistles, hawkweeds and wild carrot on most of the cliff tops and sometimes great bushes of the wild burnet rose as well. I have a notion you will like it here – and it's quite safe now – the giants have all been dead for some years!

And that is about it – as far as this enchanting land of wooded estuaries and grey stone ports is concerned. Because, tomorrow we shall make all comfortable sail that *Kala Sona* can carry and hope for a steady sou'wester to blow us straight to Chichester where after a good party at *The Ship* at Itchenor, God willing, we hope to take you on the last of this present series of wanderings, into some old haunts along the Sussex and Kent coasts before we explore the Medway and the Southern shore of the busy Thames; so, until then, good sailing.

Bibliography

Pilot Books

The Cruising Association Handbook, Cruising Association 1971.
Adlard Coles, K., *The Shell Pilot to the South Coast Harbours,* Faber & Faber 1968
Pooley, D.J., *West Country Rivers,* Yachting Monthly.

General Reading

Bradford, Ernle, *Drake,* Hodder & Stoughton, 1965.
Cowper, Frank, *Sailing Tours Part II, The Nore to the Scilly Isles,* L. Upcott Gill, 1909.
Harper, C.G. *The Dorset Coast,* Chapman & Hall, 1905.
Hay, David and Joan, *No Star at the Pole – A History of Navigation,* Charles Knight, 1971.
Holland, Clive, *From the North Foreland to Penzance,* Chatto & Windus, 1908.
Lern, Richard and Tarter, Clive, *Cornish Shipwrecks Vol. I,* David and Charles, 1969.
Mattingley, Garrett, *The Defeat of the Spanish Armada,* Penguin Books, 1962.
Norway, Arthur H., *Highways and Byways in Devon and Cornwall* Macmillan 1919.
Price Edwards, E., *The Eddystone Lighthouses,* Simpkin Marshall & Co. 1882.
Stamp, L. Dudley, *Britain's Structure and Scenery,* Collins 1946.
Steers, J.A. *The Sea Coast,* Collins 1953.
Trueman, A.E. *Geology and Scenery,* Penguin Books 1949.
Publications of the Tor Mark Press, Truro including:-
Cornish Folklore: Cornish Legends:
Cornwall's Southern Coast: Flowers of the Cornish Coast:
Birds of Cornwall, Sea and Shore: Cornwall's Ports and Harbours.

Index